Appeasement and Rearmament

APPEASEMENT AND REARMAMENT

Britain, 1936–1939

James P. Levy

ROWMAN & LITTLEFIELD PUBLISHERS, INC.
Lanham • Boulder • New York • Toronto • Oxford

ROWMAN & LITTLEFIELD PUBLISHERS, INC.

Published in the United States of America
by Rowman & Littlefield Publishers, Inc.
A wholly owned subsidiary of The Rowman & Littlefield Publishing Group, Inc.
4501 Forbes Boulevard, Suite 200, Lanham, Maryland 20706
www.rowmanlittlefield.com

PO Box 317
Oxford
OX2 9RU, UK

British Library Cataloguing in Publication Information Available

Library of Congress Cataloging-in-Publication Data

Levy, James P., 1965–
    Appeasement and rearmament : Britain, 1936-1939 / James P. Levy.
        p. cm.
    Includes bibliographical references and index.
    ISBN-13: 978-0-7425-4537-3 (cloth : alk. paper)
    ISBN-10: 0-7425-4537-7
    ISBN-13: 978-0-7425-4538-0 (pbk. : alk. paper)
    ISBN-10: 0-7425-4538-5
    1. Great Britain—Politics and government—1936–1945. 2. Great Britain—
Defenses—History—20th century. 3. Great Britain—Foreign relations—
1936–1945. 4. Great Britain—Foreign relations—Germany. I. Title.

    DA578.L444 2006
    327.4104309'043—dc22   2005026904

Printed in the United States of America

♾™ The paper used in this publication meets the minimum requirements of
American National Standard for Information Sciences—Permanence of Paper for
Printed Library Materials, ANSI/NISO Z39.48-1992.

Contents

Acknowledgments   vii

Introduction   ix

Chapter One
The Twenty-Year Truce   I

Chapter Two
1936   2I

Chapter Three
Rearmament   57

Chapter Four
1937: Chamberlain   87

Chapter Five
1938: Munich   I07

Chapter Six
1939: To War   I25

Chapter Seven
Epilogue: 1940   I45

CONTENTS

Chapter Eight
Conclusion   157

Bibliographic Essay   173

Index   179

About the Author   189

ACKNOWLEDGMENTS

I WOULD BE REMISS if I did not make public my debts to those who have helped me write this book. What understanding I have in the field of British history I owe to the mentoring of Professor Michael Simpson, now retired from the University of Wales Swansea. My many conversations with Martin Jones of Brighton, England, were also of enormous help to me in reformulating the history of the 1930s in my own head from accepted wisdom to the perspective I have adopted here. Professors John Krapp and John Teehan of the School for University Studies, Hofstra University, generously took time out to read parts of the typescript and provided many useful comments and edits. Special thanks go out to Dr. Nick Sarantakes of Texas A&M University and Dr. Michael Barnhart of the State University of New York at Stony Brook for opening the door to this project, and to Matthew Hershey and Laura Gottlieb at Rowman & Littlefield for giving me the opportunity to write this book the way I saw fit. Michael Barnhart has been a particularly astute editor and a source of valuable support and advice.

On a personal note, I wish to thank my wife, Kristine, and my children, Grace and Joe, for their support. I owe much gratitude to the authors I discuss in the bibliographic essay that concludes this book. I have mined their rich veins of scholarship and am in their debt. However, all mistakes herein are mine and mine alone. I make no claim to original research in this book, only to a distinct interpretation of the evidence. Lastly, warmest thanks go out to my parents, Jean and Ed Levy, to whom this book is dedicated.

INTRODUCTION

SINCE THE 1940S, AN OVERWHELMING CHORUS of politicians, historians, and laymen have been complaining about the "failure" of Britain and France to "stand up to Hitler" in the 1930s. Of course, they did stand up to him. Britain and France went to war against Nazi Germany in the first week of September 1939 before either Britain or France was attacked. They did it to punish Hitler for his unprovoked invasion of Poland that same week. But coming to the defense of Poland has been denounced as too little, too late. Most of the criticism of British and French action (or inaction) has been put forward in hindsight. Often, people in Britain who had not born the responsibility of sending their country into another world war made the case against Britain's pre-war leaders. Or, the case for the prosecution has been made by Americans who did nothing at the time to stop Hitler and, in fact, waited for Hitler to declare war on the United States on December 10, 1941, before wholly committing their nation to his destruction. For many, the policy of Appeasement,[1] the attempt by Britain (and France) in the 1930s to solve their disputes with Nazi Germany through diplomacy rather than war, has become a synonym for weakness, blindness, and even cowardice. This negative assessment of Appeasement is, this author believes, too harsh and simplistic. It smacks of what in American football is called "Monday morning quarterbacking." Knowing what Hitler did later, the critics of Appeasement condemn the men who tried to keep the peace in the 1930s, men who could not know what would come later. This condemnation of those who supported Appeasement as wrongheaded or deluded is unfair and inaccurate. The political leaders responsible for Appeasement made many errors. They were not blameless. But what they attempted was logical, rational, and humane. They tried to avoid a war that would, they were sure, kill an unknown (but huge) number of people, wreck Europe, and bring Britain's world position crashing down, no matter what the outcome. The supporters of Appeasement took a risk that had to be taken, and it eventually blew up in their faces. Does this failure invalidate their policy? This book will argue no.

The term *appeasement* is commonly understood to refer to a diplomatic policy aimed at avoiding war by making concessions to another power. A more technical definition from political science is: "The reduction of tension between the two sides [of a dispute] by the methodical removal of the principal causes of conflict and disagreement between them."[2] Historically, appeasement is a normal part of international relations; most countries throughout history have had to appease their more powerful neighbors. Nations have used appeasement to avoid war because the timing of the conflict was not right, domestic conditions precluded the initiation of hostilities, or the weaker nation had no chance to win. One can see appeasement in operation when Japan was forced to open her ports to American trade in 1854 or in the case where the United States backed down when confronted by British threats of war over the seizure of Confederate diplomats aboard the British merchant ship *Trent* during the American Civil War. Later, Britain adopted a policy of appeasement when it became evident that, despite the Clayton-Bulwer Treaty, which stipulated that any canal linking the Atlantic and Pacific would be a joint U.S./U.K. endeavor, the United States was going to build the Panama Canal unilaterally. Since only war could stop the United States from building a canal across Panama, and Britain figured in the early 1900s that the United States was a country she wanted as a powerful new friend, in a classic act of appeasement, the British conceded to the U.S. abrogation of the treaty.[3] A more recent example was when the United States ousted Boutros Boutros-Gali as secretary general of the United Nations. All of the members of the UN Security Council wanted Boutros-Gali to stay on—that is, aside from the United States. The American government at that time owed a billion dollars in back dues, did not want him, and made it quite plain that it was unlikely to pay up or cooperate with the United Nations if he was reappointed. The Egyptian diplomat's appointment as secretary general was not renewed. The other major powers, overawed by American power and American money, gave the Americans what they wanted—they appeased the United States.

So, why, if appeasement is such a normal part of international relations, does it have such a bad reputation when it is applied to British foreign policy in the years leading up to World War II? How has Appeasement in the 1930s become a watchword for cowardice, incompetence, and treachery? The short answer, of course, is that, because the nation being appeased was Nazi Germany, this condemnation of Appeasement sounds very moral and rather convincing: Wasn't Hitler a very evil man who murdered millions of people? Why would anyone want to grant him concessions? When one considers the matter further, the obvious point that Hitler had not killed millions of people in the 1930s pops to mind, but we shall save that issue for this book's conclusion.

Overall, the author will put forward an argument in favor of the policy of Appeasement. I will try to explain what British government officials were thinking in the 1930s and the environment in which their ideas were formed. We will see how the British came to use Appeasement as one tool in their efforts both to avoid a repeat of World War I and to solve the terrible strategic dilemma their country faced in the 1930s, with three aggressive powers—Germany, Italy, and Japan—all threatening expansion by force. Britain lacked the economic and military means to defeat all three. Her only reliable ally was France, and she was wracked by political divisions and economic hardship. Together, Britain and France were trying to maintain a fragile world order. In the end, they lacked the power to do it. Their policies must be seen in the context of this relative economic weakness and a world economy in the vice grip of the Great Depression, with the additional factor of Britain's own economy being stuck in a cycle of industrial decline. We will also consider how Appeasement was only one facet of Britain's approach to the situation, the other being a serious Rearmament program.

Before we can fully comprehend Appeasement's bad reputation, we must consider who got to write the history of those times. It is said that success has a thousand fathers, but failure is an orphan. Appeasement was certainly not a success. Although he had not been in charge when the policy was first implemented, Neville Chamberlain, who assumed office as prime minister of the Conservative government in 1937, had been a dominant British political figure throughout the 1930s. Chamberlain had held the key post of Chancellor of the Exchequer under Prime Ministers Ramsey MacDonald and Stanley Baldwin. He was to be the man who flew to Munich to try to secure peace in 1938. It was Chamberlain who made the promise to Poland and was forced to declare war against Germany in 1939. He oversaw the mobilization of British forces and was blamed for the defeats of 1940. And, critically for his future reputation, Chamberlain died in November 1940. He was not around to defend himself when the history of the 1930s got written after World War II. Winston Churchill, who opposed Appeasement, was very much alive after the war and enjoyed what this author sees as a fantastically inflated reputation. It was Churchill, starting in 1948, who wrote the first draft of the history of his times. Of course, he wrote his history of the 1930s with only one hero in mind—himself. Churchill accomplished the astonishing feat of casting himself as both John the Baptist, the prophet in the wilderness, and Jesus Christ, the savior of his country, in the summer of 1940 when all others had failed, and all was lost. Those who followed in Churchill's footsteps accepted his perspective. They also went much further than Churchill in their attacks on Chamberlain. Chamberlain became the collective whipping boy of a British establishment that was desperate to distance itself from what had been an overwhelmingly popular policy back in the 1930s but had failed to avert war and looked pathetic in retrospect. All of Britain's post-war leaders, Left and Right, wanted to bask in the glow of victory (even if that victory had largely been won by the Soviets and Americans) and not to explain how they had been complicit in Appeasement or had failed to articulate any credible alternative to it back in the 1930s. As Andrew Gordon has astutely observed about Chamberlain, "Not since Richard of York [King Richard III] has popular history so uncritically deferred to the defamation of an English national leader by his successors and their camp-followers."[4] The horror of the Holocaust gave this distancing and repudiation an ex post facto (after the fact) justification. A certain take on the events of the 1930s, one that blames everything that went wrong on Chamberlain and Appeasement, was established early, and it has stuck to this day.

It must be kept in mind that hand in hand with Appeasement went a serious, though often forgotten or underplayed, effort at rearmament. Historians lacking insight into British military and economic planning have often undervalued the effort made to arm against Hitler. They have failed to understand that a rearmament program could not and should not just throw money at the problem of relative weakness. The British could not simply print pounds or hike taxes in the middle of an economic depression. The United Kingdom was a trading nation; rapid inflation and a devaluation of the pound would have reduced its international purchasing power and made rearmament tougher, not easier, as it would have driven up the price of imported goods without which Britain could not have survived. Also, to rearm is one thing, but to choose what weapons you are going to arm your military with is quite another. A rush to rearmament in the mid-1930s would have frozen in place the production of weapons that would have been obsolescent in 1939–1940. Early attempts at arms buildups by France, Italy, and the Soviet Union seem to have hurt those countries early in World War II, not helped them, because they were burdened with an abundance of weapons one generation behind the steep technological curve.

It is important before we begin our discussion of Appeasement and Rearmament that we not forget that the evil of Nazi Germany was real. Its actions in the period between 1939 and 1945 are justly infamous. But we make a fundamental mistake if we read history backward. The Holocaust had not happened yet when Appeasement was official British government policy. The evil of Stalin's Russia was much more apparent in those years than the full villainy of Nazi rule. It is usual to date the opening salvo of the Holocaust to *Kristallnacht*, the night when Nazi thugs were let loose to burn down synagogues and smash the windows of Jewish shops. Thousand of German Jews were terrorized that night, many were beaten, and over a hundred were killed. But Kristallnacht took place in November 1938, two months after the Munich Agreements, the high water mark of British prime minister Neville Chamberlain's Appeasement policy. By March of 1939, that agreement was unraveling, and on September 3, 1939, Chamberlain took his country to war over German aggression against Poland. Historical events happen in sequence, and, as we all know from our own lives, the future is unknown territory. British prime minister Neville Chamberlain wanted to solve the problems of his day, not throw up his hands and surrender to the inevitability of what everyone knew would be a devastating war. He was neither passive nor defeatist. For Chamberlain, Germany was the problem, and if that problem were to be solved, Germany had to be engaged in a dialogue. As a reasonable man, Chamberlain tried negotiation first and saw the use of violence as a last resort. Again, this is nothing new in international relations. It also conforms to most conceptions of the prelude to a "just war." Two questions dominate most inquiries as to whether or not a war is just: Have all efforts to resolve the dispute short of war been taken? Will the continuation of peace cause more harm than the war itself? Before September 1939, the answer to both questions was almost certainly "No." Therefore, a strong case can be made that Appeasement was morally defensible before the invasion of Poland. But to understand how Britain in the 1930s got to a place where war looked likely and Appeasement seemed the only sound course of action, we have to go back to the end of World War I and see how the Allied leaders at Versailles failed to secure a lasting peace.

NOTES

1. Throughout this book the words "appeasement" and "rearmament" will be capitalized when they refer to the specific government policies.

2. Definition from Gordon Craig and Alexander L. George, *Force and Statecraft* (New York: Oxford University Press, 1995), 247.

3. For the Clayton-Bulwer Treaty, see Paul Kennedy, *The Rise and Fall of British Naval Mastery* (London: Ashfield Press, 1986), 212.

4. G. A. H. Gordon, *British Seapower and Procurement between the Wars* (Annapolis, MD: Naval Institute Press, 1988), 288.

Chapter One

THE TWENTY-YEAR TRUCE

ON NOVEMBER 11, 1918, AN ARMISTICE was signed that mercifully stopped the fighting and effectively ended World War I. As the smoke of battle cleared, the United Kingdom of Great Britain and Ireland found itself with the largest navy, the largest air force, and one of the largest armies on Earth. The sun never set on the British Empire. A vast mobilization of manpower, money, and industry under the dynamic leadership of Prime Minister David Lloyd George had contributed mightily to Allied victory over Germany, Austria-Hungary, and the Ottoman Empire. Britain was well placed to influence the organization of what was fervently hoped to be a peaceful, prosperous post-war order. But errors, ill will, and unforeseeable circumstances were to render all the hopes of that peace of exhaustion moot. Instead of a stable world order, a twenty-year truce would ensue. If we are to understand the origins of the policies of Appeasement and Rearmament, we must go back to the end of World War I and the attempt to patch together a viable peace after four devastating years of war.

One might assume that victory and shared sacrifices would have cemented bonds of friendship and trust among the Allies. They did not. During the war, British industry had supplied weapons to America and Russia, and British loans had kept France and Italy in the war. But, by 1916, Britain had been forced to seek her own loans in the United States. Although the French, Russians, and Italians owed Britain more money than Britain owed the Americans, the chance of any of those countries paying their debts was somewhere between slim and none. Yet, the victory of 1918 had been a collective effort. Troops from Australia and New Zealand were crucial in breaking the back of the Turkish Army. French and Serbian soldiers had exploded out of the Salonika bridgehead and driven Bulgaria from the war. Italian troops pursued the routed, demoralized Austro-Hungarian forces in the Veneto. On the western front, Americans were, by the autumn of 1918, carrying an equal share of the burden so long borne by the French, British, and Canadians. American food and cash now backstopped the Allied war effort. The victorious Allies had weathered the storm and now reaped the fruits of victory. But, every combatant except the United States, because she entered the fighting so late, had run down its economy and run up too many debts. Europeans hoped that their greater sacrifices in terms of blood—1.4 million dead Frenchmen and 700,000 dead Britons, compared to 100,000 dead Americans—would lead to a forgiveness of their debts by the United States. Nevertheless, the Americans wanted their money back. So, when the Allied leaders got together at the Versailles Palace outside Paris in the winter of 1918–1919 to hammer out a peace treaty, every Allied delegation was as concerned about how they were going to pay for the war as they were about figuring out how to cement a peace. Distracted by debts, tied to promises made to their electorates about the sweet fruits of victory, shackled to assurances expressed to the Italians, Arabs, and Jews to induce them to fight on the Allied side, and complicit in wartime anti-German propaganda, the Allied leaders had little room to maneuver and failed to take the steps necessary to solidify a peaceful post-war world. The Allies' obligations and constraints led to several mistakes in formulating a sustainable settlement.

After such a bitter war, how was victory to be made sweet? The Allied leaders hit upon the idea of having the Germans pay for it all. Germany would be presented with an immense bill for reparations. Reparations were payments of money and goods that the Germans would have to disgorge as restitution to the Allies for the cost of the war. Germany was also to be stripped of all her overseas colonies and her substantial modern navy. The deal was made nonnegotiable. Agree to our terms, the Allies said, or we will continue our devastating trade blockade and send in troops to occupy Germany itself. To justify these reparations, the Allied leaders put a "guilt clause" in the treaty that said, in effect, the total responsibility for starting World War I rested with Germany. The Germans hated this. They argued that it was the Austro-Hungarians who had begun hostilities by attacking the Serbs. The Austrians had done so because the Serbs had backed the terrorists who killed the heir to the Austro-Hungarian throne. Therefore, the Austrians had legitimately declared war on the Serbians. In response, the Russians had mobilized their forces in support of Serbia, which threatened Germany and her ally Austria-Hungary. Germany then either had to fight or abandon her only loyal ally, the Austro-Hungarian Empire. These were valid points, if a bit too flattering toward the Germans. Germany was very much to blame for starting World War I; however, there was plenty of blame to go around, especially in Vienna, Belgrade, and St. Petersburg. Nevertheless, the Germans had lost the war, and their army had fallen apart after the armistice. They got what the Allies wanted to give them, which was a bill for billions in reparations, and the German government was forced to agree to a "confession" of guilt. Reparations were finally fixed at $131 billion, a number so astronomical in those days as to be virtually meaningless; by comparison, the entire output of the German economy in 1937 was only $17 billion.[1] The Allied demands for enormous reparations, along with an admission of war guilt, would breed animosity across the political spectrum in Germany and create some of the resentment Adolf Hitler and the Nazis were so skilled at exploiting. And, in the end, it proved impossible to force the Germans to pay regularly or in full. Thus, the Allies got all of Germany's rage and little of her money.

When Germany defaulted on her reparations payments in 1923, the French Army marched into the Ruhr, Germany's industrial heartland. They tried to collect their reparations in goods rather than cash. German workers declared a general strike, and industrial production ground to a halt. Furious and frustrated, the French withdrew back over the Rhine. Their act had looked to most people like aggression. Germany was bankrupt and obviously defenseless. France was trying to kick Germany when she was down, making Germany look like the victim of French bullying. To make matters worse, in addition to being a public relations fiasco, the invasion had accomplished nothing. Germany was further alienated from the victors (if that was possible). In the likely event that the Germans would not forget this insult, France asked Britain and the United States to guarantee her border with Germany, just in case the Germans one day decided to pay the French a return visit. Both Britain and

America refused. The French responded by hunkering down in a defensive posture, worried about the future and unable to see a clear way either to live in peace with the Germans or to defeat them single-handedly in war.

Whether or not it was a mistake is debatable, but to mollify the French, the Versailles Treaty limited the German Army to six thousand officers and one hundred thousand men. To placate the British public, the once-mighty German Navy was handed over as reparations to the Allies. The Germans were allowed to keep a few obsolete, pre-*Dreadnought* battleships, light cruisers, and torpedo boats for coastal defense. Germany was denied the right to have an air force, heavy artillery, poison gas, or tanks. She was not only rendered incapable of offensive military operations, but she could no longer even defend herself. One can imagine how poorly this was received in Germany. As a sop to public opinion everywhere, which was, by 1919, increasingly anti-war, a clause was thrown into the treaty stating that Germany's disarmament was only a prelude to general disarmament among all of the major powers. This never happened. So, after Hitler came to power, he would renounce the limitations on German armaments and invoke the failure of the Allies to honor the disarmament clause in the treaty as justification. For many people in 1935, it seemed he had a legitimate case.

A clear mistake that the Allies made at Versailles was the creation of the "mandate" system. Territories that had belonged to Germany and Turkey as parts of their empires were transferred to the Allies. These territories were portrayed as areas needing the tutelage of Western powers that could bring them a dose of "civilization"; in actuality, they were the spoils of war, compensation to the Allies, especially the South Africans, Australians, French, and Japanese—another form of reparations. But in Britain's case, two of these territories,

Palestine and Iraq, were to prove poison pills, with local in-surrections in both places tying up British money and military resources in the inter-war years. The mandates were effectively a fig leaf cloaking imperialism and smacked of hypocrisy. It was patently disingenuous to harp on the evils of German im-perialism and aggression, then to turn around and gobble up her colonies. One did not look good in the process. Mandates added another level of illegitimacy to the already questionable proceedings at Versailles.

Further mistakes were made. The Allies announced in the treaty that a League of Nations was to be formed to set-tle disputes between nations without resort to war. Then, they shunned Germany by not including her new, democrat-ically elected Left-Liberal government in the League. The fi-nal mistake was in forcing all this humiliation not on the kaiser's government, which had collapsed, but on the new German government that was filled with the people who had pushed the kaiser into abdication in 1918. The Allies wanted to punish Germany and ignored the fact that the men forced to sign the Treaty of Versailles on June 28, 1919, were not the people who were pulling the levers of power in 1914. The shame of agreeing to what most Germans considered a com-pletely unfair peace deal accrued not to the kaiser, who was off in exile, or to the Germany military, which had backed him, but to the democratic government that signed the Ver-sailles Treaty. German democracy was tainted in many eyes from this point, and a return to authoritarian rule in Ger-many became a real danger. Nothing that happened at Ver-sailles excuses the actions of Germany later on, but it was unwise to foster conditions in a defeated power that made the rise of fanatics like Hitler more, not less, likely and increased the chance of a future war. Sometimes, it may prove better to be wise than to be just, or fair, or simply popular.

In summation, the Versailles Treaty achieved relatively little toward creating a viable post-war international order. It did not actually end the war—that had come with the armistice. It gave France back the provinces of Alsace and Lorraine, which they had lost to the Germans in 1871. Britain was relieved of the dangerous headache that was the kaiser's High Seas Fleet. Woodrow Wilson got his League of Nations, which his compatriots immediately repudiated. Italy received a few extra miles of Alpine rock and ice at the expense of the Austrian Empire, which had ceased to exist. The Arabs got three puppet kingdoms under British tutelage (Saudi Arabia, Transjordan, and Iraq), sliced from the carcass of the dying Ottoman Empire. The Jews got a quota of immigrants for Palestine. Japan got some coral atolls. Germany lost about 5 percent of her pre-war territory, her unspectacular overseas colonial empire, and her rather impressive navy; received a huge bill for reparations; and was forced to admit guilt for World War I. The Austro-Hungarian Empire was split into Austria, Hungary, Czechoslovakia, and Yugoslavia. Poland reemerged as an independent nation after over a century of German, Austrian, and Russian partition. The Ottoman Empire completely disintegrated. Perhaps nine million people had died in the conflict. After such upheaval, and on this shaky foundation, the post-war order was constructed.

For Britain, any future problems with a disgruntled Germany would have to wait. In the short run, Germany was bankrupt, disarmed, and in a state of social and political chaos. Britain's big problems at hand in 1919 were the guerrilla war in Ireland, agitation for home rule in India, confrontation with the Bolshevik revolutionaries in Russia, continuing trouble with Turkey, and an impending naval arms race with America and Japan. With Germany eclipsed, the British could ignore events in Central and Western Europe for the time being. Prime Minister Lloyd George had promised to make Britain "a nation fit for heroes," which meant additional domestic spending on housing, schools, and hospitals. His country had incurred massive debts in waging World War I. Something had to give. Defense spending was cut drastically. A "Ten Year Rule" was imposed, stating that, for budgetary purposes, the British armed forces were to assume that no major war would be fought for the next ten years. Later, Winston Churchill, while serving as Chancellor of the Exchequer, would convince the Cabinet that the Ten Year Rule should be considered to be in effect automatically during each fiscal year until the Cabinet revoked it formally. Belatedly, efforts to intervene militarily against the Bolsheviks were abandoned, a negotiated settlement was reached with the Irish Nationalists in 1921, and, after a show of force in the Bosporus, an agreement was reached over free passage into and out of the Black Sea with the new Turkish government. Britain was curtailing her overseas obligations and retrenching her strategic position. Overseas commitments could not be allowed to outstrip financial resources, but the problem of growing American strength and assertiveness would have to be dealt with. The anxious situation of creeping mistrust and hostility between Britain and the United States over war debts and a nascent naval arms race was serious, and it was compounded by rifts between Britain and her dominions: Australia, New Zealand, and Canada.

The British Empire and the United States were the greatest economic and military powers after World War I. Their potential rivalry generated tension. If a showdown with the United States came, Britain's only reliable ally of military importance was Japan (New Zealand would almost assuredly stand by England but would not count for much). Britain and Japan had signed a military alliance in 1902, and Japan had supported the Allied cause in World War I. But American animosity toward Japan was already a matter of record. Asian exclusion laws barred Japanese immigration to the United States; the U.S. Navy devoted most of its planning to an anticipated future war with Japan. America had imperial possessions in the Pacific—the Philippines, Guam, and Hawaii—and great faith in the viability of the China market, a market Japan wished to capture for herself. Attitudes and interests on both sides put the two powers on a collision course. Japan and the United States had begun massive naval building programs in 1916, just when Britain stopped building battleships (with the exception of the big battlecruiser *Hood*) to devote steel for destroyers to protect against U-boats and for artillery and tanks for the western front. Now, with the war over, Japan and the United States kept on building. Britain would soon be forced to respond if she was to maintain her lead. A major arms race, which Britain could not afford, and perhaps could not win, loomed on the horizon.

In addition, Britain's dominions were sending strong signals to London that they wanted a change in British policy. Australia and New Zealand were afraid of Japan and wanted Britain to guarantee their interests in the Pacific, even at the cost of the Anglo-Japanese alliance. Canada wanted the United States appeased at all costs as Canada would be the front line in any Anglo-American war. Britain herself saw Japan as a rival for markets in Asia. It looked as if Britain might have to choose between her ally Japan and the continued loyalty of her dominions. Then, President Warren G. Harding of the United States changed the global strategic situation completely. He called for all of the major naval powers to gather in Washington, D.C., to discuss Pacific Ocean affairs and naval arms limitations.[2]

Harding was motivated, as are almost all American presidents, by internal political factors in his calling for an international naval arms limitation conference. He needed a prestigious foreign policy success to give him some gravitas and dispel his small-town, Ohio, rube persona. The presidential vote in 1920 was probably as much a rejection of the Wilsonian Democrats as it was a warm embrace of Harding. Harding also had to appease his Republican base by cutting taxes and balancing the budget, the two pillars of pre-Reagan Republican orthodoxy. Big navies meant hefty taxes, and that implied a continuation of high wartime tax rates that were unacceptable to Wall Street and innumerable chambers of commerce. A naval arms treaty could kill two birds with one stone.

The Washington Naval Conference got off to a spectacular start. The Americans proposed sweeping cuts to the battlefleets of all of the major powers, a building "holiday" during which no new battleships were to be built for ten years, and limitations on the size of new cruisers and aircraft carriers. To top this off, the total tonnage (the size of warships is measured in the number of tons ships weigh) of battleships allowed to each power was to be capped at a fixed ratio of 5:5:3:1.76:1.76. This meant that Britain and the United States would each be allowed up to 525,000 tons of battleships, Japan would get 315,000 tons of battleships, and Italy and France would get 176,000 tons each. Because different ships weighed in at different tonnages, the number of ships was not always exactly the same as the tonnage ratio (Britain got 21 ships, the United Staes 18, Japan 10; in 1930 the ratio was reset at 15, 15, and 9 battleships, respectively). To seal the deal, the Americans demanded the termination of the

Anglo-Japanese military alliance. The Anglo-Japanese Treaty was of great benefit to Britain. It confronted the Americans with the nightmare of having to fight a naval war in both the Atlantic and the Pacific simultaneously if they chose to attack the United Kingdom or its possessions. It made it possible for the British to station only token forces in the Pacific in peace-time; the Japanese could "cover Britain's back" in that ocean, thus saving Britain a lot of money that could be better spent on ships and supplies. For exactly these reasons, the Americans wanted the alliance ended.

Since the Americans had opened the conference with such a comprehensive plan, negotiations were largely taken up with points within the established American framework. The British delegation was not prepared for what the Americans had proposed, and the Americans stayed one step ahead of their "guests" by intercepting and decoding their secret communications. The Americans set the rules of the game, and everyone was compelled to play along. All of the major powers wanted the conference to succeed. But at what cost?

The British Admiralty was stunned and appalled by the American proposals. The treaty would hand away British naval supremacy. Britannia would no longer rule the waves; she would have to share them. Great Britain was an island nation completely dependent on overseas trade for her survival. The United States was a continental state only marginally dependent on overseas trade at that time. Yet, the Americans were adamant—they wanted parity and an end to the Japanese alliance, and they threatened to build toward superiority if they did not get both. In retrospect, the Americans were probably bluffing, but the British could not be sure of that. The British government believed that war with the United States would be an economic catastrophe and could at best be fought to a draw. An arms race with America could not be won. For financial and strategic reasons, Britain would have to concede parity. Japan would have to be abandoned. At the cost of keeping the Americans friendly, the British sacrificed naval superiority and their alliance with Japan. The first great act of British appeasement between the world wars was directed at the United States, not Germany. Very soon, the Admiralty would be planning for a war not with the Japanese but against them. "Instead of the Anglo-Japanese alliance, based upon the nice calculation of mutual interests and relative capacities, Britain was to enter into a new system whose functioning would principally depend upon the incalculable shifts and whims of the American democracy."[3] The Japanese were furious at the British for dumping them and at the Americans for assigning them second-class status in ship tonnage. But without British support, Japan had no option but to sign.[4] The Washington Treaty, like the Treaty of Versailles, was intended to secure peace. Unfortunately, like Versailles, it did much to sow the seeds of a future war. The treaty's stipulations forced British strategic thinking to fixate on imperial security. The huge army of 1918 was demobilized, and thoughts of a future Continental commitment of forces fell into abeyance. Without absolute naval superiority, British military policy became circumspect. The British Foreign Office summed up the nation's strategic outlook in one clear sentence: "Our sole object is to keep what we have and live in peace."[5] In the 1930s, the desire to keep what Britain had and live in peace would remain the guiding principle that informed Appeasement. The British had had their "glorious crusade" in the "war to end all wars." Now, they just wanted to be left to recover something of the affluence and security they had enjoyed in the days of Queen Victoria and King Edward VII.

The period following the Washington Naval Conference was marked by the peace and prosperity most Ameri-

cans associate with the Jazz Age. Economies everywhere re-
covered from the strains of World War I. Business and trade
boomed. Yet, Britain enjoyed, as best we can ascertain from
the economic statistics of that time, the least robust recovery among the major powers. When Britons looked out at
the world, some circles felt a keen anxiety about a new political movement on the Right, fascism, which had taken over
in Italy in 1922. But the threat of communism, which had
looked so menacing to the British establishment in
1919–1920, was subsiding as the new Soviet leader, Joseph
Stalin, concentrated on building "socialism in one country."
From Wall Street to Paris to Tokyo, times were good. The
United States and France organized the Kellogg-Briand Pact
renouncing the use of war as an instrument of foreign policy, and most nations signed on. At Locarno, Italy, in 1925,
Britain, France, Germany, Italy, Belgium, and Czechoslovakia
all agreed to recognize and respect each other's borders. Another naval disarmament conference was due to commence
in 1930, although an earlier general disarmament conference
in Geneva in 1927 had failed to accomplish anything and
ended in bitter acrimony between the United States and
Great Britain over cruiser tonnage and numerical parity. Despite this minor setback, for a few years, it looked as if the
peace and prosperity of 1896 to 1911, which many men
and women could still remember with the greatest fondness,
had returned. Economic growth rates in the Americas, Australia, and much of continental Europe were high, and new
consumer goods like automobiles, radios, and refrigerators
started to spread to a wider and wider middle-class clientele.
Republican presidential candidate Herbert Hoover in 1928
told his people that the end of poverty in America was in
sight. Americans were even promised "a chicken in every
pot." Jazz Age prosperity was, however, not to last. The place

where it disappeared first, and where its consequences were to be most extreme, was in Germany.

Parliamentary democracy had stabilized in Germany after the turmoil and economic hardships of 1919 to 1923. But during those years, a decorated war veteran of Austrian extraction, Adolf Hitler, had made a name for himself when he and some ragtag followers had tried to overthrow the government of the German state of Bavaria in 1923. He wound up serving a year in jail after his coup came to nothing, and most of his support evaporated in the good times that followed. But by 1928, the German economy was sputtering. In October 1929, the U.S. stock market crashed. Credit tightened. Unemployment rose everywhere as sales dropped and trade diminished. For example, the value of European trade fell from $58 billion in 1928 to $20.8 billion in 1935.[6] The more people lost their jobs, the less purchasing power was generated in the economy. Falling demand meant less need for products, so ever more people were laid off from work. Business inventories grew, and profits fell. Nations with democratic political systems were forced to respond to the rising tide of poverty, but the social welfare measures enacted to meet public need caused government expenditures to rise just as tax revenues were falling because of decreased economic activity. The world economy spiraled downward into the Great Depression.

By the time the major powers got together for the London Naval Conference in 1930, their objective was as much to cut government spending as it was to control the growth of armaments. Italy and France were so worried about each other's navies that they could hardly agree on anything. The United States, Great Britain, and the empire of Japan agreed to continue the battleship-building holiday for another six years. The United States insisted that total British cruiser tonnage (which had not been regulated at Washington) be restricted so that it would be more in line with U.S. strength (the Americans at that time had far fewer cruisers than the British). The Admiralty complained that this would leave Britain with too few cruisers to guard her vital sea lines of communication. America did not have a worldwide empire to protect. However, the idea of parity had become so important to Americans' self-image that the Hoover administration could accept nothing less. The Labour government, which had no great love of military spending in the first place, was not disposed to put up a fight. The British economy was in terrible shape. The U.S. economy had grown much faster in the 1920s than had the British economy, so, despite the Depression, America was in a better position to outspend Britain in an arms race in 1930 than she had been in 1920. Thus, Britain again chose to appease the United States in the hope that, when push came to shove, in any future conflict, American sea power would be on Britain's side. The British got a compromise tonnage ceiling below what they really needed and later built small cruisers to stretch that tonnage over more hulls; the Americans got near parity in total tonnage but never built up to the limit. Honor was satisfied, and expenses were cut. German nationalists continued to rage against the Versailles Treaty's military restrictions and insisted upon a place within the global arms control matrix consistent with Germany's economic and demographic standing. Their assertions were ignored.

The results for the Royal Navy of the London Naval Treaty were serious. The vital shipbuilding industry was hard hit. Naval building in Scotland, England, and Northern Ireland practically came to a stop. British battleships were, on average, older than those of the United States and Japan, and these aging ships could not now be replaced. The Royal Navy was only allowed fifty cruisers when it needed seventy, so fewer were built than had been projected. Cancelled contracts meant idle shipyards and layoffs. Merchant ship construction also collapsed as international trade diminished; if goods are not moving, merchants do not need ships to carry them. Unemployment rose as shipyards lost orders. Many skilled workers left the yards for good, seeking employment in other industries or even overseas. This would create a serious deficiency of skilled manpower that would take considerable time and effort to remedy when the decision to rearm was made in 1936.

The Great Depression was the central event for much of the world in the period from 1929 to 1936. The depression brought back the popularity of the Nazis with a vengeance. By 1932, the Nazis and the Communists together commanded a "negative majority" in Germany's parliament. Voting as a block, they could defeat any legislation. Although they hated each other, the Nazis and the Communists both had an interest in wrecking German democracy. Both felt that economic disaster and political deadlock would create the conditions under which they could take power. German chancellors, with the support of the largely figurehead president, took to ruling by decree. This was legal under the German constitution in a national emergency, but after a certain set time, the decrees had to be approved by parliament, which then could reject them. Given Nazi and Communist obstruction, rule by decree became necessary in order to get anything done, however temporarily. But rule by decree undermined the democratic nature of German politics. It set a dangerous precedent and, in the long run, could not solve the political crisis. Many Germans wanted someone to step in and break the impasse. They would not have too long to wait.

Casting our gaze more widely, we see that in the early 1930s the Great Depression savaged the world capitalist economy. In the Soviet Union, a different set of hardships was being endured. Stalin, who had emerged from a Byzantine power struggle in the 1920s to rule Russia, had set about collectivizing agriculture. That meant taking from the peasants the farmland they had wrested from the upper class in 1917 and placing it under government control. This did not go down well with the peasants. Most of the more successful peasants, whom Americans would categorize as small farmers, actively and passively resisted collectivization. In the Soviet Union, these people were called kulaks, and Stalin set out to "liquidate" them. Millions died in the famines and fighting that followed. Millions more were shipped off to the massive complex of work camps set up in Siberia to deal with those who opposed the Soviet system, the gulags. All the while, Stalin was embarking on a vast project of industrialization. Despite everything, he pulled it off; the name Stalin does not mean "man of steel" in Russian for nothing. The tradeoff was grotesque, but the horror and death of the 1930s enabled the building of the factories that turned out the tanks, guns, and planes that did so much to defeat Hitler in World War II. It also set off a debate over who was the worse tyrant, Hitler or Stalin, which has never been resolved and probably never can be.

The United States was suffering from an estimated 25 percent unemployment and a run on the banks when Franklin Delano Roosevelt took office in March 1933. In his improvisatory way, and with boundless energy and optimism, Roosevelt stanched the bleeding. But he lacked the vision and the political leeway to vault the United States out of the Depression. His country's political culture was antithetical to radical measures like unbridled social spending. Roosevelt governed a confused and demoralized nation that had received a giant blow to its ego. In the

1920s, Republicans had assured citizens that prosperity was permanent and that poverty would soon be a thing of the past. Americans were left dazed when it all went so very wrong. Never particularly interested in foreign affairs in the best of times, in the 1930s, the American polity grew increasingly isolationist. This retreat from world affairs went back to 1919. Disillusioned by the experience of World War I, confused as to why everyone did not acknowledge America's unique virtue and natural right to world leadership, Americans had rejected the League of Nations and quickly thereafter recoiled from any responsibility for global order. Despite the rise of Hitler, and even after he had begun his wars of conquest, the United States clung to the sidelines. This isolationist stance would predominate in American politics right up to the Japanese attack on Pearl Harbor.

The collapse of the world economy generated a variety of responses. Britain and France largely tried to muddle through and hoped for better days. The United States retreated into isolationism and erected tariff walls around its shrunken economy. Soviet Russia was at once a dynamo and a slaughterhouse. Germany was off on its own road to economic autonomy under Hitler's brutal dictatorship. Japan in 1931 and Italy in 1935 turned to imperialism in hopes of solving their problems. Both nations believed that only through the colonization of excess rural population and by capturing markets and raw materials could they compete as major powers. Tensions rose. War clouds appeared on the horizon. We must now turn to the pivotal year of 1936 and see how the world situation pushed Britain toward the two key policies she would adopt in hopes of riding out the crisis: Appeasement and Rearmament.

NOTES

1. Statistics are from B. J. C. McKercher, *Transition of Power* (Cambridge: Cambridge University Press, 1999), 17, and Paul Kennedy, *The Rise and Fall of the Great Powers* (New York: Vintage, 1989), 332.

2. For the preliminaries, see Roger Dingman, *Power in the Pacific: The Origins of Naval Arms Limitation, 1914–1922* (Chicago: University of Chicago Press, 1976).

3. Quotation from Paul Kennedy, *The Rise and Fall of British Naval Mastery* (London: Ashfield Press, 1986), 276.

4. Kennedy, *British Naval Mastery*, 274–83.

5. Quotation from Michael Simpson, *A Life of Admiral of the Fleet Sir Andrew Cunningham* (London: Frank Cass, 2004), 19.

6. Kennedy, *Rise and Fall of the Great Powers*, 284.

Chapter Two

1936

Our year of departure for exploring the policies of Appeasement and Rearmament is 1936. This year was the pivot point of the inter-war period. Even a cursory review of the salient events of 1936 clearly demonstrates how bewildering and dangerous the times were. In 1936, Hitler sent troops into the demilitarized Rhineland, Benito Mussolini conquered Ethiopia (at that time called Abyssinia), the Spanish Civil War erupted, and France saw the electoral victory of a Leftist coalition led by a Jew, Leon Blum, that badly split an already divided polity. In that same year, Britain was rocked by a constitutional crisis that led to the abdication of King Edward VIII, and Russia endured the first year of Stalin's Great Purge. Every major power was faced with both internal and external crises and distractions. If, today, we attribute primacy of importance to the rise of Hitler's Germany, that fact was not so clear at the time. That Hitler would precipitate a second world war in only three years was too fantastic and dreadful to appear credible. Everything seemed to be in flux. Britain and France, who in 1935 had signed with Italy the Stressa Agreement aimed at containing

Germany, suddenly, in 1936, found Italy drifting into the German camp in the dispute over Italian aggression against Ethiopia. Public opinion in Britain and France made a close relationship with Italy impossible so long as her armies ravaged Ethiopia. Italian Fascist dictator Benito Mussolini needed a friend. Hitler was glad to embrace him at a time when Britain was forced to turn its back on Italy.

Spain's Civil War between her Leftist government and Hard Right army had repercussions far beyond the Iberian Peninsula and polarized the political landscape worldwide. The battle over Spain's future seemed like the harbinger of a global showdown between supporters of "socialism" and "fascism" (loosely defined). Like some terrible, lingering illness, the world economic depression would not go away. Tariff wars stifled international trade. The Versailles Treaty's supposed answer to such turmoil, the League of Nations, looked on, impotent. Already, in 1931, the Japanese invasion and occupation of Manchuria had marked a serious breach of the post-Versailles global order. The Italians had seized the port city of Trieste from the Yugoslavs in 1921, and the French had temporarily occupied the Ruhr in 1923, but these had been localized events and their repercussions were quickly smoothed over at Locarno. However, cracks in the Royal Navy's vaunted discipline, revealed in a refusal by sailors facing pay cuts to go to sea, and Japan's decision to absorb a region over six times the size of Great Britain could not be ignored. Under the league charter, an attack on any member should have triggered a diplomatic, economic, and, if judged serious enough, military response from other league members. Yet, the League's response to Japanese aggression was feeble. A fact-finding mission was sent out to observe the situation, investigate the conflicting claims of the Japanese and Chinese, and recommend a course of action. While the league dithered, the Japanese smashed the Chinese and grabbed what they wanted. Confronted with a fait accompli, the league folded. No nation was prepared to come to China's aid. Forcing the Japanese out would mean a full-scale war half way around the world from Britain and France, the only two nations with the naval forces that could intervene in the Far East. They lacked the political will, public support, and financial resources for such a venture. Effectively, collective security under the rubric of the league was a dead letter. However, league members would continue to tiptoe around the corpse of collective security for some years, not daring to bury the body and acknowledge the real situation, that no international mechanism existed to deal with military aggressors. Five years later, with Italian troops bombing and gassing their way through Ethiopia, calls for collective security and league intervention would be heard again. But the obvious fact was that the major powers were not going to act to protect the rights of weak states far away. The league's authority had been flouted when Japan invaded Manchuria in 1931, and its protests had been brushed aside by Italy in 1936. Without the United States or Nazi Germany among its members, and without any consensus within its own ranks, the league became moribund. The United States further undermined the league by refusing to cooperate with the League of Nations in any program of economic sanctions against Italy to punish her for devouring Ethiopia. The international political and economic order, barely patched together in the mid-1920s from the damage inflicted by World War I, lay again in ruins. For the statesmen of the day, these were indeed bewildering and dangerous times.

In this chapter, we take a close look at three nations—Britain, France, and Germany. As this is a book about Appeasement and Rearmament as the United Kingdom practiced them, our tightest focus is on the United Kingdom. We look at Britain from a social, economic, political, and strategic perspective with special emphasis on the domestic and international situation in 1936. Shorter sections follow dealing with France and Germany. After re-creating in this chapter the setting in which Appeasement and Rearmament functioned, we devote the following two chapters to a detailed discussion of these two key policies: Rearmament in chapter 3, then Appeasement in chapter 4.

Britain in the 1930s was a land of stark contrasts. It was a nation of cities and countryside; 80 percent of the population lived in urban areas of fifty thousand or more, mostly in London and the great industrial cities of the nineteenth century: Manchester, Birmingham, Leeds, Sheffield, Newcastle, Cardiff, Belfast, and Glasgow. Few suburbs had yet developed. The vast tracts of suburbia that post-1950 Americans take for granted and the burgeoning middle class that populated them did not exist. Thus, the divide between town and country was pronounced. The rich still led a life of enviable opulence with servants and country houses. The urban poor lived in grimy, polluted slums, often in substandard housing without central heat, hot water, or even indoor bathrooms. Britain was still overwhelmingly a Christian country, but most citizens no longer attended church on Sundays, and the old laws that had once forced attendance were gone from the books. Yet, the dominant position of the established Church of England remained in force. Anglican bishops sat in the House of Lords, and, by law, an Anglican sat on the throne. But with a general fall in religious observance and the removal of "Anglicans-only" laws, the great tripartite religious divide in British life between Anglicans, Catholics, and non-Anglican Protestants (the "Nonconformists") was ebbing in importance. The loss of much of

Catholic Ireland in 1922 with the founding of the Irish Free State confirmed this diminution of the importance of religion in British life. Britain was becoming a "postreligious" society; its ethos was very different from the creedal passions and prejudices that had shaped British social life and politics from the time of Henry VIII to the pre-1914 battles over Irish home rule. In place of religion came a greater and greater emphasis on class distinctions.

Money, in the last analysis, is nearly always at the root of class distinctions. This was true, of course, in Britain in the 1930s. However, the barriers to economic advancement were not as great as they had once been, when class was largely an issue of birth. The elite were still almost exclusively male, Anglican, and Oxford or Cambridge educated. But Britain was not completely caste bound. You need look no further than the careers of three prime ministers of that era to see that advancement, even from humble origins, was quite possible. Prime Minister David Lloyd George came from rural Wales, could actually speak Welsh, was a Methodist, and never attended university. Ramsay Macdonald's father was from the working class. Neville Chamberlain was raised a Unitarian but became a skeptic on religious matters and went to the University of Birmingham, not Oxford or Cambridge. What had replaced the overt snobbery of birth was increasingly the more covert division of society by education. This would perhaps have been equitable if merit determined access to schooling, but it did not. British education was distinctly unequal for rich and poor.

Although most people were literate, Britain was an undereducated society by the standards of America or Germany in those years. The leaving age for students from school was fourteen, and few children of the working class, or even the lower middle class, were educated beyond that point. Before poorer children left to join the workforce, their parents sent them to local government primary schools that were not richly endowed with staff or amenities. The curriculum stressed reading, writing, and arithmetic. Better-off middle-class parents often sent their boys (and a smattering of their girls) to grammar schools once they reached the age of fourteen. These academic-oriented secondary schools were open to all who could pass the competitive entrance examinations and pay the fees. Graduation from a grammar school opened up careers in management and the civil service and was essential if you wanted to go on to university. Open access to grammar schools sounds egalitarian, but, in practice, it was not. Most working-class families needed their kids to start earning a living by the time they were fifteen (Britain was, by twenty-first-century American standards, a very poor country in 1936). So, few families could spare the child's income, and fewer still could pay the fees to send their children to a grammar school. A modest number of scholarships helped the brightest of the lower-class boys get a proper education and partially hid the fact that the system was so grossly unfair.

Rich people sent their boys (and increasingly their girls) to expensive boarding schools that taught them the Latin and history they needed to score well on university entrance exams. Practicality was not an issue at these so-called public schools; the watchword was "character." This the boys would show by being good sports and keeping a stiff upper lip, having the right accent and pronunciation, and doing just enough hard work to get by. Science was not part of the core curriculum, and although British scientists racked up an impressive score of Nobel prizes in the first half of the twentieth century, an infrastructure of engineers and technicians was not properly developed. Fine universities had been founded at London, Manchester, and Birmingham and, of course, had existed for centuries in Scotland, but Oxford and Cambridge alumni dominated the "old boys" network (a term which originally indicated a man's having once been a boy at one of the elite boarding schools) that controlled admission to the upper echelons of society and government. Exclusive clubs and the marriage patterns of the upper class buttressed the whole system. Outsiders could break into the inner sanctum, but it was damned difficult. Only one student in a hundred at Oxford and Cambridge came from a working-class background. These inequalities were exacerbated by an economy that simply refused to grow quickly enough to raise the overall standard of living and move large numbers of people into the middle class.

The British economy suffered from serious structural problems that went beyond the fact that it was mired in the Depression. In every mature economy, a tension exists between keeping the value of the currency up to support the financial sector and letting the value of the currency slide against other currencies to make industrial exports cheaper for foreigners and therefore more competitive in world markets. Since the 1890s, the drift in the British economy had been in favor of the financial sector and against the industrial sector. Britain was the center of international trade, banking, and insurance. Her stock market was, along with Wall Street, the center of international finance. All trading nations valued their goods in British pounds or gold, and the pound was firmly based on the gold standard; you could at any time trade in your pounds for the equivalent value in gold. To maintain the value of the pound, British governments had to make sure that the flow of funds into Britain was positive, that at the end of each year, Britain made more money on her exports, banking charges, shipping fees, repatriated profits, and insurance premiums than she exported in payments for foreign goods and services. If she did not, then Britain would have to reach into her gold reserves to cover the deficit. Since Britain had only so much gold, such a policy was unsustainable.

After World War I, Winston Churchill, at that time Chancellor of the Exchequer (the cabinet minister in charge of government budgeting and finance) in the Conservative Cabinet, made a fateful decision. Britain had been temporarily forced to suspend gold payments during World War I. Churchill put Britain back on the gold standard at an exchange value of £1 being worth $4.86 in American currency. This exchange rate was too high. It overvalued the pound. To float the pound at that rate, Churchill had to keep government expenditures down. He pushed hard for cuts in the navy's budget, which were approved, and disparaged the navy's contention that Japan was a long-term military threat.[1] Churchill later changed his tune (when he no longer held office), but the damage was done.

The overvalued pound helped restore confidence in the British financial sector, but it made British exports very expensive at a time when British industry, sapped of strength by the exertions of World War I and stuck with antiquated Victorian plant and equipment, was having trouble recapturing foreign markets. This led quickly to a vicious cycle: British exports were noncompetitive, so the balance of trade between imports and exports grew. Soon, Britain was forced to sell off foreign currency reserves, and later gold, to cover the imbalance. Chronic balance-of-trade deficits made it difficult to keep up the value of the pound against foreign currencies, so Britain had to reach deeper into her reserves to prop up the pound.

The more the British pound looked like it was sliding, the more money Britain had to spend to prop up its value.

In 1931, the situation exploded. People saw the writing on the wall and started demanding gold for their pounds. They thought that the exchange rate could not last and wanted to cash in before the value of the pound dropped. The Labour Party government was faced with a run on the pound. They tried to bring spending under control and to balance the budget through pay cuts to government workers and by slashing unemployment insurance benefits. If the government did not have to borrow money and showed its "fiscal responsibility" by taking whatever measures were deemed necessary, then maybe faith in the pound would be restored. Most Labour Party members hated this plan. The Labour prime minister, Ramsey Macdonald, was convinced by his economic advisors and by the Bank of England that drastic cuts in government spending would prevent a suspension of the gold standard and save the pound. He was forced to seek support from the Conservative and Liberal parties to push through the cuts. The Labour Party kicked Macdonald out, and many of his cabinet ministers resigned rather than support the cuts to workers and the unemployed. However, the king asked him to stay on as prime minister in a coalition "National" government. Meanwhile, all hell was breaking loose. The Atlantic Fleet went on strike over the pay cuts. Japan invaded Manchuria, and the British stood by, impotent. The run on the pound did not abate. The British economy tanked. Britain went off the gold standard and let the value of the pound "float." This helped as a weaker pound made British exports more competitive and eased unemployment as some factories went back into production, but Britain's position as the financial hub of the world economy was dealt a fatal blow. Faith in the pound as "the" currency of international exchange was shattered. The British economy would make a sluggish recovery; growth was slow and unemployment remained high throughout the 1930s. The repercussions of the dual financial shocks of 1929 and 1931 were to have far-reaching implications for Britain's ability to face the threat of war later in the 1930s.

The fall of the city of London as the center of the global economy would not have been as bad if the British industrial sector had been in better shape to compensate for the lost revenue. The British economy had been built on coal, textiles, pottery, iron goods (knives, forks, railroad tracks, ships), and the reexport of colonial products like sugar and tea. But growing competition from Germany and the United States had been eating into British global market share for years. Britain had accounted for 14.15 percent of world trade in 1913. By 1937, she was down to 9.8 percent of the Depression-shrunken pie. British industrial production in 1938 was 17.6 percent above what it had been in 1900; German industry had grown 49 percent since 1900, while U.S. industrial production jumped 43 percent.[2] After World War I, the advanced economies were converting from coal-powered steam engines to oil-fired electric generators. Mass production techniques were being introduced, especially in the United States. Chemical industries were coming into their own, and Germany was the dominant player in chemicals and also precision instruments. The automobile and the truck were becoming important forms of transportation. In all of these fields, Britain lagged behind. Worse still, her key exports, coal and textiles, were either no longer in demand or no longer competitive with foreign producers. Many British firms tended to be small, family-owned enterprises or partnerships and lacked capital for both expansion and research and development. Most catered to the home market, which was still underdeveloped compared to the United States, where even during the Depression you still had some·vestiges of the consumer economy of the 1920s. The British upper class preferred to invest in government bonds or more profitable foreign firms rather than in British industries with their poor return on investment and chronic labor strife. So, plant and equipment were run down. The huge investments that had been made in industrial plant by Germany and the United States during the 1920s had barely begun in Britain before the Depression hit. The British would find in the 1930s that they would have to retool industry before they could rearm their defense forces, while Hitler and, later, Roosevelt would reap the benefits of a larger and more modernized industrial base.

In certain areas, like aircraft engines, electronics, and pure science, Britain was at or near the top of the list of world leaders. But in chemicals, engineering, machine tools, and consumer goods, the British were at best mediocre. It is no accident that the British word for vacuum cleaner is "Hoover." It is more serious to contemplate that one reason for the poor performance of British shipboard antiaircraft guns during World War II was that they did not have stabilizers to compensate for the pitch and roll of the ship. They lacked them because stabilizers need gyroscopes, and British industry could not supply enough of these high-tech gadgets. Before World War II, many had to be purchased abroad—from Germany! Although British industry was able to produce radar and sonar sets, Spitfire fighters, and excellent artillery and antitank guns, Royal Navy ships were only average in quality, British tanks were poor, and British production techniques were labor intensive and comparatively inefficient. Most importantly, British industry was smaller and weaker than its German counterpart. And for Britain's politicians, the fact of German industrial superiority colored every calculation from 1936 on. But we must take a closer look at British politics if we are to understand something about the actions of British politicians; thus, it is to British political life that we must now turn.

Britain was more or less a democracy in 1936, in some ways more so than the United States. Unlike the United States, where blacks were almost completely disenfranchised after 1896, enough Catholics already had the vote in Ireland by 1918 to give Sinn Fein an absolute majority in the twenty-six counties that became the Free State. By 1936, virtually all adults over the age of twenty-one had the vote. Up until 1918, there had been property or tax requirements for voting. Before 1918, if you were a man and did not own property or pay enough in taxes, you could not vote. And, as in the United States in those days, women could not vote. World War I changed all that. Since during World War I every adult male had been liable to serve king and country, as had a fair number of women, it became impossible to defend restrictions on the franchise. The law was changed in 1918, and all adult males and many women over thirty got the vote. In 1930, Parliament granted all women the vote. So, by 1936, a higher percentage of Britons could vote than Americans.

In national elections, turnout hovered around 75 percent of the electorate, but in local elections, fewer people went to the polls. Most offices were held by "respectable" members of the community. As in the United States, this meant lawyers, bank managers, local landowners, and businessmen. The only difference between the United States and the United Kingdom was the number of younger sons of the aristocracy who served as Conservative Party members of Parliament (MPs). In Britain, if you had a title of nobility, you could not vote in general elections; you got your vote in the House of Lords. But younger sons of the nobility did not inherit titles and, therefore, could and often did sit in the House of Commons.

Britain's unwritten constitution was a hodgepodge of laws and customs that directed the way government operated. Britain still had a king and a House of Lords, but these institutions had been in decline for over a century. The mythical power of the absolute monarch (British monarchs had never held absolute power) had been transformed by 1936 into reality in the form of the House of Commons, which had almost absolute power within the realm. The House of Lords could delay legislation and force Commons to vote again on bills they did not like, but if Commons voted yes twice, the bill passed. The king, in principle, still had veto power over legislation, but Queen Anne had been the last monarch to veto a bill in 1706. So, the checks and balances written into the U.S. Constitution did not apply in Britain. Almost everyone had the vote, the people could read a diverse and largely free press, and the courts were independent and miraculously free of corruption, but the House of Commons had the power to change any or all of these things if it wanted to. The habit of freedom prevailed without formal guarantees of freedom as Americans have enjoyed in the Bill of Rights. In criminal law, juries and judges had limited powers to check Parliament's will by refusing to convict people under unpopular statutes. But in national and foreign policy, the House of Commons had the last say on everything. The power of the House of Commons was unchallengeable.

By law, the House of Commons had to face the electorate at least once every five years. The prime minister, however, could ask the monarch to dissolve Parliament at any time and call for a general election. By tradition, the leader of the party with the most seats in Parliament was called on by the monarch to form a government. If no party had a majority, the king or queen had to choose someone he or she thought could form a coalition and command a working majority. In either case, the new prime minister would put together a Cabinet. The Cabinet was often, in those days, made up of powerful figures in Parliament who had their own followers within the majority party. They might also be men with special skills that the prime minister needed. Although prime ministers were powerful figures, they could not make decisions willy-nilly. They needed firm support from key cabinet ministers and from their party's MPs. In 1936, Prime Minster Stanley Baldwin was in no way the dominating chief executive that modern American presidents are.

Prime ministers expected and usually got the full support of the MPs from their party. Party discipline was strict, and if you won an election, your party was in charge. As long as you commanded a majority in the House of Commons and your cabinet and MPs backed you, prime ministers ran the country and got what they wanted. In this way, although a prime minister as an individual was weaker than a U.S. president, the prime minister, working together with the Cabinet and the MPs, was collectively stronger.

Britain in the 1930s had three major political parties: Conservative, Liberal, and Labour. Throughout the 1800s, Britain was largely a two-party political culture divided between Liberals and Conservatives. Those labels do not correspond with how people define "liberal" and "conservative" today. Nineteenth-century British Liberals championed free trade, limited government, low taxes, a small military establishment, and, usually, a more pacific foreign policy. Liberals also opposed the Anglican Church's influence on public education and championed the rights of Nonconformists and occasionally those of Catholics. Most wanted greater rights granted to the people who lived in Ireland. Their power base was among industrialists, those in the financial sector, the educated middle class, and members of the Nonconformist churches. The Conservatives usually supported tariff barriers to protect the home market, the power of the Anglican Church, the prerogatives of the monarchy, and a more aggressive foreign policy. Their base of power was among the land-owning class, the aristocracy, and the rural populace. However, after World War I, the two parties started to merge. Some of the drift of Liberals into the Conservative Party was due to rival personalities and splits among the Liberals. The followers of Herbert Asquith and the followers of David Lloyd George hated each other and divided the Liberal Party. As the division made it impossible to form a Liberal majority in Parliament, it no longer paid to stand for election as a Liberal or to join a party that had little chance of ever forming a government. Another factor was that the Liberals were the victims of their own success. They had won the day on free trade and nonsectarian public education. Catholic Ireland was now gone, so home rule was no longer an issue. But, mostly, the Liberals were the victims of the rise of the new Labour Party. For, in the end, Liberals and Conservatives represented two competing views of a capitalist and hierarchical society. Each party was run by men of wealth and property. Many Liberals and virtually all Conservatives viewed the rise of a working class party with alarm. Many of the more "reformist" Liberals went over to Labour. Many more of the better-off Liberals saw the Conservatives as the surest bulwark against the "Socialist" rabble. British politics became more polarized. Instead of opting for a middle-of-the-road alternative, by 1945 people had largely aligned themselves with the Left and joined Labour or with the

Right and gone to the Conservatives. The powerful old Liberal Party was almost completely destroyed in this political-electoral realignment.

The British political system was wracked by a silent crisis, largely kept quiet by an acquiescent press, throughout much of 1936. On January 20, 1936, King George V died. A stern and upright father figure for his countrymen, he had held the respect of all parties because he was seen as solid, fair, and content to abide by his constitutional role as confidential advisor to the prime minister. George V's son and heir was the bright, flighty, earnest Edward, Prince of Wales. Stanley Baldwin thought him too callow to take his father's place, having too many opinions he rather indiscreetly shared with the press. Worse, he had gotten himself tangled up in a love affair with a twice-divorced American, older than him and of exceedingly common origins. Mrs. Wallis Simpson was still married to her second husband when she began sleeping with Prince Edward. Now, with his tough old father out of the way, Edward intended to marry Wallis Simpson. Baldwin, Neville Chamberlain, his right-hand man and obvious successor as prime minister, and the archbishop of Canterbury, who was religious head of the established Church of England, were unalterably opposed to the marriage. They thought it indiscreet, childish, and a shocking indictment of the future king's judgment. Winston Churchill rallied to the king's defense, but this only hurt his standing among the political elite. Baldwin presented Edward with a clear choice: dump Mrs. Simpson or abdicate. Edward waffled. He asked if Parliament could pass a law saying that he could take the throne, but Wallis Simpson would not become queen, only a princess. Baldwin consulted the dominion prime ministers, since Edward would be king in Canada, Australia, New Zealand, and South Africa, as well as in

Great Britain and Northern Ireland; they all rejected the idea, as did he. The story finally hit the newspapers. A full-blown constitutional crisis erupted. Baldwin, so often slow and taciturn, became a man possessed. He wanted Edward VIII to choose—immediately. Churchill rose in the House of Commons to beg for King Edward to have time to consider his options but was derisively howled down. Edward abdicated on December 11, 1936. He was replaced by his brother Prince Albert, the Duke of York, who took the name King George VI. Thin, frail, high strung, and afflicted with a stammer, George VI would go on to become a dutiful and very popular monarch. But the many months spent securing the throne for him and unseating his controversial elder brother had distracted the government from much more important work, the job of keeping the British Empire's strategic head above water.

In simplest terms, Britain's strategic dilemma in the 1930s could be summed up as follows: too many potential enemies, too few resources to keep them all at bay. Germany, Italy, and Japan all wanted a piece of the British Empire, or they directly threatened British interests, or both. The Soviet Union was an unlikely, but far from unimaginable, enemy. The United States was a completely unreliable quasifriend. Only France could be counted on if the chips were down in Europe to stand by England. And, sadly, France was no match for Germany in an even-up contest. So, from London, the world looked like, and very much was, a dangerous place.

Britain in the 1930s was, as it is termed in political science, a *satisfied power*. By "satisfied," political scientists mean content with the international system as it exists and averse to changing it. By contrast, states unhappy with the division of power and prestige within a given international system— in the 1930s, Italy, Germany, and Japan—are referred to as *revisionist* because they wish to revise or change the international political order. Britain in the nineteenth century had captured everything her wit, skill, and economic base were capable of wresting from the world. She was the center of the world diplomatic order and enjoyed great prestige. Her fighting men commanded respect, and she had a navy second to none. But, at heart, Great Britain was a small island nation with few natural resources, dependent on imports to survive, with a stagnant economy and a middling population. By 1938, the United States, Germany, and the Soviet Union all had larger populations and bigger economies. Britain had exploited her lead in the industrial revolution to the full, but now that lead was gone, having passed to other nations. How long Britain could retain her place among the Great Powers (at that time defined as Britain, France, the United States, the Soviet Union, Germany, Japan, and Italy) was of growing concern to the men in London who guided her destiny.

The British Empire was past the point where it was a collective asset; many of its parts were, by the 1930s, a growing liability. They cost more to police and protect than the British could extract from them. Like a weary sheepdog watching a huge, heterogeneous flock, Britannia was all too well aware that the wolves were lurking close by and that she had but two eyes to watch for them and not enough teeth to keep them all at bay. Or, as Paul Kennedy has phrased it, Britain suffered from "imperial overstretch"; her resources in money and manpower were no longer sufficient to guarantee the security of her many possessions. What to defend and where to draw the line against aggression became the British government's overriding defense policy questions after 1933. In chapter 3, we focus on British defense policy in those years, but first we must take a look at Britain's only reliable ally, France, and her greatest likely enemy, Germany.

Because of the deep wounds inflicted on the French nation by World War I, French national policy was, much more than Britain's, dominated by defense policy. Over one million Frenchmen had died in the trenches, and large areas of northern France had been completely destroyed in the war. So, everyone was concerned about issues of war and peace and the potential threat of a revivified Germany. But divisions within the French electorate stymied French military policy after World War I. France, since the 1870s, had been a constitutional republic, dominated by the usual suspects in such regimes: lawyers, businessmen, and landowners. She also had a residual aristocracy, a fair number of very conservative priests, an equal number of anticlerical writers and teachers, a large class of small farmers and agricultural laborers, and an industrial working class. On the most practical level, these divisions were manifested in the seventeen parties that divided up the 615 seats in the Chamber of Deputies in 1938. This made stable coalitions difficult to form. It also meant that consensus was absolutely essential (since no group commanded a majority) but tough to hammer out on controversial issues. French politicians, like British ones, could not ignore the electorate, and France's was a deeply disunited one. In the 1920s, an attempt was made to put future national war-mobilization plans on a sound legal and administrative footing. A law was drafted that would have solidified the existing eighteen-month period of universal conscription for males, allowed for the conscription of women for war work, and placed French industry and the wealth of Frenchmen at the disposal of the government for use, even expropriation, in wartime. If, or when, war came, all France would be expected to sacrifice for the common cause. Political reality, however, slammed headlong into this lovely, logical plan.

On the Right, politicians were appalled at the idea that their daughters would be dragged off to work in grubby factories next to washerwomen and prostitutes. They also demanded that private property should be respected and capitalists be allowed to make a profit off of government contracts, even in wartime. On the Left, the demand was simple: if men were to be conscripted, so should wealth. The nation needed bodies, but it also needed cash. Should the capitalists not be soaked to pay for war while the workingmen spilled their blood on the battlefield? The sides were irreconcilable. The Chamber of Deputies passed one bill (largely representing the ideas of the Left), and the Senate passed another (one can guess which side they were on). The government realized that the two bills were incompatible and let the whole thing drop. There the matter rested. When Hitler came to power in 1933, France had no coherent plan for national mobilization.[3]

Yet, French opinion was generally consistent on two issues: the majority of people did not want war and the majority of people were not prepared to capitulate domination of Europe to Germany to prevent war. Even Leon Blum's Left-Liberal Popular Front Government of 1936–1938, which was seen as ideologically committed to peace and disarmament, followed the same script: arming against possible German aggression while seeking ways to avoid war. French foreign policy was, in this way, remarkably consistent, whether men of the Left or the Right were practicing it. Although divided on many social and ideological issues, France retained certain coherent foreign policy goals. The question in the 1930s was, how could France avoid war, retain her Great Power status, avoid ruining her economy by overspending on defense, and keep Germany in check, all at the same time. The answer French political leaders came up with was very much the same as that reached by the British—conciliation toward Germany to see if she could be persuaded by reason, rearmament as insurance if conciliation failed. Yet, despite this similarity between British and French policies for dealing with Germany, a fundamental discrepancy of interests plagued the two powers throughout the 1930s. France could never escape her proximity to Germany, whereas Britain could not ignore her empire and dominions. Britain was content to see Holland, Belgium, and France remain independent. France needed and wanted alliances with Poland, Czechoslovakia, and, if possible, the Soviet Union to overawe Germany and keep her quiescent. Britain wanted nothing to do with Eastern Europe. In fact, Admiral of the Fleet Lord Chatfield, while acting as chairman of the Chiefs of Staff Committee, privately hoped that Germany would turn eastward and become entangled in conflict with the Soviets. The whole Anglo-French relationship was riddled with these discrepancies. They would have made Allied coordination very difficult even if the personalities had gotten on well, which they did not. One such discrepancy arose over relations with Italy. France always wanted to win her over, while the British waffled. When news that the French had argued for a rapprochement with Italy at the expense of Ethiopia reached the British public, there was a storm of protest. The British people did not want war over Ethiopia, but they also did not want to cut humiliating deals with a nation like Italy that they looked down upon as a bunch of disreputable and inferior gelato makers. The French believed that if the British would not cut a deal with Italy, they should at least give France a guarantee that, if war came, Britain would fight alongside France. The British government would not, however, give France any such ironclad guarantee of support. British political leaders feared that France would go off half-cocked and drag Britain into a war she did not want or need. The British never understood that France wanted a formal military alliance not to start a war but to prevent losing one if it ever came to a showdown with Germany. Likewise, attempts by France to get her other democratic friend, the United States, to give her assurances of support if she were the victim of an unprovoked attack went nowhere. France was stuck with weak or fickle friends and a powerful, implacable foe. Her leaders were overwhelmed and confused. To whom do we turn for help? How do we deal with Hitler? As one prominent historian of the period has commented, French policy was driven not by fear but by ambivalence, a feeling that the circle could not be squared.[4]

Things slid along unresolved until the threat from Germany became all too real. The French Army formulated its own plans for war without coordinating with industry or society at large. Eugenia Kiesling has brilliantly summed up the French Army's answer to the German challenge: "Faced with the likelihood of renewed German aggression, France produced the long-war strategy. Needing a military doctrine appropriate to her military institutions, France developed the methodical battle."[5] As in Britain, French military leaders believed that for economic reasons (a lack of raw materials and of gold and foreign currency to pay for them, even if they were attainable through an Allied blockade), Germany was likely to lose a long war. The French and British empires (France always counted on British support if she were to fight successfully against Germany) would provide the raw materials and extra manpower that would tip the scales against Germany, which was bigger in industry and population than France or Britain. In a total war, in which societies mobilized their whole strength to defeat their enemies, Britain and France together, given time to harvest the resources of their overseas empires, would hold the preponderance of power and prevail. This, it was argued with justification, had been the recipe for defeating Germany in World War I: mobilizing manpower, resources, and allies, while Germany was being bled to death in a war of attrition. France, reflecting on its success in 1918, thought she could do it again, with British and Belgian help, of course. But this time, the horrendous casualties that had almost destroyed the French Army in World War I would have to be avoided.

For the first three years of World War I, French soldiers hurled themselves in brave, but futile, assaults on the German trenches. By the time the war was over in 1918, about 1.4 million Frenchmen were dead. The next time, French generals decided, no such bloodletting would take place. France would stand on the defensive. Let the Germans run up against artillery, machine guns, and the new fortresses of the Maginot Line. As one expert has noted correctly about the French generals in the late 1930s: "They were men not of the distant past but of the First World War, men who had learned their lessons from it. . . . [M]ost were men who had done their principle service on the western front, where the war had settled into the mud, trenches, and fixed positions of static armies."[6] In year one of the next war, they thought, French armies would absorb the initial German offensive, just as they had in 1914. In the second year, after full mobilization and with British help, Allied armies would begin the slow process of launching limited offensives backed by massive artillery and tank support to cut out chunks of the German line and further weaken the German Army. Some time in year three or four, with Germany clearly losing, under pressure from blockade and the aerial bombing of her cities and industries, the Nazi regime would collapse, just as the kaiser's government had fallen apart in 1918. By using the tactics of the methodical battle—massive concentrations of artillery and tanks, narrow fronts, and limited objectives—heavy blows could be delivered at the minimum cost in French lives. Battles would be managed from the top with firepower substituting for bayonets or maneuver. Careful planning and plenty of preparation time for each attack would substitute for surprise and daring. That was the plan developed by the French. It was neither stupid nor unrealistic. In the long run, that is how Nazi Germany was defeated (Stalingrad, Normandy, Monte Cassino, and a dozen other examples prove the point). But it necessitated an ability to survive the initial German onslaught. This proved nearly impossible because of problems with the organization and training of the French Army and because the German Army hit upon a risky doctrine of all-out offensive operations, known as blitzkrieg, that involved deep penetration of the enemy's rear areas by tanks and truck-borne infantry. But before we can discuss what the Germans got right, we have to touch on the structural weaknesses that hindered French Army performance early in the war.

French recruits after 1929 served for only one year, then joined the reserves. France maintained many more active units than she had recruits to man them. Therefore, recruits served in what were largely skeletal formations. Divisions were made up of officers and noncoms (sergeants and corporals) from the relatively small regular army and, say, all of the twenty-one-year-olds inducted in a given year. But to reach full strength, the division would need men who were in the reserves. When war broke out, the reserves would be called up, and the army's divisions filled out to full strength. This was logical for a defensive, long-war strategy, which is exactly what the French had in mind. But it made peacetime training of large formations very difficult as the regiments and divisions existed only at partial strength. So, almost all of the training the men had took place at the platoon and company levels. Officers and men had little or no experience fighting in large combat formations or with tanks and artillery in combined-arms teams. Because of their short term of service, conscripts barely learned the basics in their accelerated boot camps. Then, they had to be hustled either into schools for advanced training with machine guns or antitank guns or into artillery or engineer units where, after only a familiarization course, their time was up, and the men were discharged into the reserves. And the reserves spent very little time on refresher courses with the units they would fight with in wartime. This meant that if France had to go to war, she would have to call up her reservists and give them and the current conscripts a long and thorough dose of training before they could do much more than guard the frontier defenses. The simple fact was that, when Hitler reoccupied the Rhineland in 1936, French organization and French doctrine made an immediate response impossible. Ironically, not only was France not surprised by Hitler's move, but she had anticipated it for so long that it did not really generate a crisis. Only in retrospect has this come to be seen as a great opportunity lost. The French government at the time only wanted to use Hitler's move into the Rhineland as a way to push the British into serious talks about what they might do if the German's crossed an international frontier. The commander of the French Army, General Maurice-Gustave Gamelin, told the government in no uncertain terms that the army could not effectively respond to the German move into the Rhineland. France's unit organization, manpower policy, and military doctrine were optimized to fight a long, initially defensive war, not a short, lighting campaign.

A few words on the Maginot Line are in order here. The Maginot Line of fortresses was started in 1928 and largely completed in 1936. These fortresses formed a series of mutually supporting strong points with artillery, antitank defenses, and infantry bunkers along the Franco-German frontier. Historians for years have ridiculed them as a waste of money and a factor in French "passivity." Most of these critics miss the mark. The Maginot Line was never intended to make France impregnable to invasion. It was built in order to limit the manpower needed to hold the border so that reserves could be spared in case troops had to be sent into Belgium. Given the inevitability of German numerical superiority (there would always be more Germans than Frenchmen), this made perfect sense. Since the Germans had come through Belgium and Luxembourg in 1914, and would again in 1940, using steel and concrete to maximize the defensive strength of those units that had to guard the Franco-German border was more than prudent; it was absolutely essential. The argument that the money would have better been spent on tanks and airplanes fails to take into account the fundamental historical factor of chronology. The Maginot Line was largely built in the early 1930s. If France had used the money to procure tanks then, they would have been worthless antiques by 1939 or 1940. The pace of aircraft and tank development in the 1930s meant that countries, like Italy and the Soviet Union, that started major arms-production programs in the period between 1933 and 1936 were saddled with obsolete or obsolescent equipment when war came between 1939 and 1941. France was better off with the Maginot Line.[7]

The French Air Force, which had been the largest in the world in the 1920s, was stuck with a large inventory of obsolete machines by the mid-1930s. It would require complete modernization, and the French aeronautical industry was not in the short run up to the challenge. A revolution in aircraft design took place in the mid-1930s as monoplanes replaced the biplanes of World War I and aircraft engine power improved dramatically. France had fallen behind the industrial and technological curve. She had exploited the technology of 1918 to the hilt but failed to keep pace after about 1925. Much time and investment was needed to make the French Air Force a match in numbers and quality for its German counterpart. The job was not nearly complete when France fell in June 1940.

Oddly, the French Navy had experienced a renaissance in the 1920s and 1930s. It had some of the best new ships afloat, and its destroyers and light cruisers were of the most modern designs. Four new battleships were proceeding from the drawing board to the builder's yard in 1939. Two new battlecruisers, far superior to Germany's three vaunted "pocket battleships," had joined the fleet in the mid-1930s. The French Navy was a great, and undervalued, asset to the Anglo-French alliance. If the British Empire were to face the nightmare scenario of war with Germany, Italy, and Japan simultaneously, the French Fleet would be as important to Britain's survival as the French Army.

All this meant that in 1936, and well beyond, France could only fight one kind of war, a long contest of attrition to a methodical plan, because France did not field a large professional army. This was so because a professional army was seen by the Left, and even by moderates, as a threat to the Third Republic. The traditional antidemocratic sympathies of French officers frightened all who held the Republic dear. People had not forgotten the Dreyfus Affair. They knew that perhaps a majority of French officers were hostile to democracy or, at best, ambivalent about it. The military had actively supported the overthrow of the First and the Second republics. Professional armies were not to be trusted. And all Frenchmen who loved the Republic looked back to the citizen-soldiers of the French Revolution with the reverence Americans in those years heaped on the Minutemen of Lexington and Concord. A majority of Frenchmen preferred that their own army, whatever its effectiveness against foreign armies, reflect the ideals of their civil society and not threaten the established democratic order at home.

France depended on conscription and the reserves to give her the numbers she needed to face Germany with its larger population and greater industrial strength. It was a cheaper system than a large, standing professional army and did not break the budget. Conscription fit the national ideology of the citizen-soldier and the strategic needs of French defense policy. Additionally, France depended on fighting a long war because it was France's best chance to win. Anglo-French naval supremacy would guarantee a blockade of Germany, British bombers would raid German cities and industries, and the German Army would be broken on the horns of the French defenses and through the steady pounding of the methodical battle. It all made perfect sense. It just did not succeed in 1940.

Hitler came to power in January 1933 through an alliance of Germany's conservative parties, of which the Nazis were only one, although it was the biggest. The traditional conservative parties, like the Nationalists, wanted to establish a more authoritarian government with the power to deal with the economic crisis of the Depression and the clout to bring the Socialists, Communists, and trade unions to heel. They wanted a return to the "good old days" of the kaiser. Respectable members of the German Right saw Hitler as a crowd-pleasing rabble-rouser who could win

The uneasy alliance: British Prime Minister Neville Chamberlain (left) and French Premier Edouard Daladier (right) in 1938. Despite the experience of cooperation in the 1914–18 War, the British and French suffered from failures of shared perception and communication in the late 1930s (courtesy of Hulton-Deutch Collection/CORBIS).

votes from the lower middle class for the aristocratic and business elites. These elites would run the show, and Hitler would be their front man. It did not work out that way. Brilliant and ruthless, with boundless ambition, Hitler quickly outmaneuvered all of the groups and institutions that could check his power.

In a titanic stroke of ill luck for civilization, a mentally retarded Dutchman, who happened to have once been a member of the Communist Party, set the Reichstag (Parliament) building on fire only weeks into Hitler's chancellorship. The aging German president, Field Marshal Paul von Hindenburg, granted Hitler and his cabinet sweeping powers to deal with this terrorist "crisis." All 81 Communist members of the Reichstag were arrested, along with 6 of the 120 who represented the Social Democrats. Brown-shirted Nazi storm troopers roamed the streets, beating and arresting opponents of Hitler. Concentration camps sprang up throughout Germany, at this time to house political prisoners. When the Nationalist Party leader, who was the deputy chancellor in Hitler's cabinet, complained in writing to Hitler about Nazi thugs looting and killing ordinary citizens, he was told point-blank to shut his mouth—he was not entitled to ask such impertinent questions.[8]

Hitler resorted not just to sticks; he dangled carrots in front of important elements in German society, too. He won over the military by promising them a rearmed Germany with promotions all around. He was not adverse to a few well-placed bribes and dismissals, either. Hitler used contracts for rearmament to buy off the capitalists, along with promises to suppress the Communists and the trade unions; no nasty labor trouble, strikes, or demands for higher wages to worry about. He reduced the Cabinet to impotence and the Reichstag to a rubber stamp. All political parties, save the Nazi Party, were banned. All organizations, clubs, and societies were taken over by the Nazi Party or outlawed. If you went along, jobs, perks, and the property of political prisoners (or Jews after 1935) were at your disposal. Resistance meant imprisonment, torture, exile, or death. Given such a stark choice, most Germans chose to conform. As economic conditions improved dramatically and street violence was curtailed, Hitler was transformed from a man who could, at best, muster one-third of the German people's vote to a respected national leader. When President Hindenburg died in 1934, Hitler stood alone as master of Germany.

The Treaty of Versailles had limited the size of the German Army to six thousand officers and one hundred thousand men. Only a token navy and no air force were permitted. Germany could not produce tanks or poison gas. Instead of lamenting, in the 1920s the army set to work on building an elite cadre force that could form the nucleus of a much larger army. The officer corps was pruned down from the huge numbers of 1918. Only the best men were kept. With serious post-war unemployment, the army always had more volunteers than places in the ranks. Everyone was trained to do his own job and the jobs of officers or non-commissioned officers two steps in rank above his own so that Germany would have a large number of highly trained professionals when the government sanctioned rearmament. Lessons from the defeat in World War I were learned, and a highly aggressive doctrine that placed authority to take the initiative in the hands of junior officers was instituted. Attacks were to depend on surprise, infiltration behind enemy lines, and rapid exploitation of any success to put the enemy physically and psychologically on the defensive. This doctrine of surprise, breakthrough, and rapid exploitation was in place even before the tanks that were to make it so deadly were deployed in the German Army. German generals understood that they could not win a long war of attrition, so they adjusted their strategy to taking risks in order to ensure quick, knockout blows against their enemies. They built up the army very rapidly after 1935 and concentrated on what is termed rearmament in breadth rather than rearmament in depth. The idea was to put as many troops in the front lines as possible, along with almost all available equipment. Stockpiles were not built up so that combat formations could have as many tanks, trucks, and guns as possible. Everything was gambled on hitting a future enemy (Poland?

France? Czechoslovakia?) so hard and so fast that the war never bogged down into a contest over mobilization and resources. German strategy came down to this: win the battles quickly, and the war will take care of itself.

The salient event for Germany in 1936 was the reoccupation of the Rhineland. Although everyone recognized the Rhineland as part of Germany, the Treaty of Versailles forbade Germany to station troops in this territory, so close to the French frontier. Hitler decided to send troops in to reassert German sovereignty. He had already initiated conscription and the creation of an air force, both forbidden by the Versailles Treaty. He had publicly declared Versailles dead. He guessed nobody would do anything about it. Hitler sent an infantry division (about ten thousand men) into the Rhineland on March 7, 1936. He mobilized four divisions of trained policemen and border guards to back them up. He kept another two divisions close at hand, just in case. This was not the inconsiderable force that it has often been made out to be. Britain at that time could cobble together two divisions from units at home to intervene on the Continent. Obviously, this was not going to do the trick. France's coalition government had recently collapsed, so Paris was in no state to act decisively. Her army was not designed for such a contingency. France could mobilize her army, but then what? Hitler could do the same in his country, and he would still have the Rhineland. Much of the Royal Navy was in the Mediterranean in case war broke out with Italy over her invasion of Ethiopia. Nobody wanted millions to die over the Rhineland. The idea that this was some "golden opportunity to stop Hitler," the standard anti-Appeasement line, is untenable. It takes no account of the military realities of the time, the political situation in Britain and France, the fact that Britain's overseas dominions (Canada, Australia,

New Zealand, South Africa) were unlikely to back England in an "offensive" war, or the effects of public opinion in a democracy. As Hugh Dalton, one of the few Labour Party leaders fully committed to opposing Hitler, said at the time, "Public opinion in this country would not support, [*sic*] the taking of military sanctions or even economic sanctions against Germany at this time."[9] Or, as historian Michael Howard so memorably put it, British politicians were terribly conscious of "the heavy and ominous breathing of a parsimonious and pacific electorate."[10] Germany certainly was not ready for war in 1936, but neither was Britain or France. All arguments against Appeasement are predicated on the assumption that if war came in 1936 or 1938, it would have gone better for the Allies than it did in 1940. A serious look at the British and the French armies does not lend much support to such an assumption.

To everyone's chagrin outside Germany, Hitler had won a public relations victory. He had shown courage and determination when his generals had urged caution and nearly panicked. Most Germans were proud of his action and his performance. Hitler understood that after World War I, the threshold for resorting to war had risen. It was going to take more than a simple provocation to push nations over the precipice and into another world war. Very few people anywhere wanted a repeat of the rush to war in 1914. Even Hitler covered his tracks by stressing in his public utterances his desire for peace and made assurances that his goal was the restoration of Germany's sovereignty and honor, not war. He said repeatedly that he only wanted for Germany to be allotted the same rights and respect as any other nation and that all Germans should be able to live in one German nation-state. Hitler's real desire was for an alliance with Britain that would cow the French and leave him a free hand to conquer "living space" in Eastern Europe. Poland, Czechoslovakia, and the Ukraine would supply him with land for colonization and the raw materials necessary for Germany to take her place at the forefront of the Great Powers. To Hitler, the British Empire was a bulwark of white supremacy; its dissolution could only aid Japan and the United States, not Germany. If he could reach a properly advantageous understanding with Britain, so much the better.

For the rest of 1936, Hitler pushed German rearmament despite an overheated economy that threatened to explode into runaway inflation, bided his time, and looked for his next opportunity for personal and national aggrandizement. Meanwhile, in London, the British government was in search of a defense policy to deter war and, if Appeasement failed, to fight Hitler's Germany and beat it.

NOTES

1. Andrew Field, *Royal Navy Strategy in the Far East 1919–1939* (London: Frank Cass, 2004), 29, 234.

2. Statistics from Paul Kennedy, *The Rise and Fall of the Great Powers* (New York: Vintage, 1989), 299, 316.

3. Eugenia Kiesling, *Arming against Hitler* (Lawrence: University of Kansas Press, 1996), 12–24.

4. Robert J. Young, *France and the Origins of the Second World War* (New York: St. Martin's Press, 1996), 7–13.

5. Kiesling, *Arming against Hitler*, 6.

6. Robert J. Young, quoted in Ernest May, ed., *Knowing One's Enemies: Intelligence Assessment before the Two World Wars* (Princeton, NJ: Princeton University Press, 1984), 300–301.

7. An excellent introduction to the Maginot Line is William All-corn, *The Maginot Line 1928–45* (Oxford: Osprey Books, 2003).

8. For Hitler's power grab, see Alan Bullock, *Hitler and Stalin: Parallel Lives* (New York: Vintage, 1991), 302–9.

9. Quotation from A. J. P. Taylor, *English History: 1914–1945* (Oxford: Oxford University Press, 1965), 386.

10. Quotation from Paul Kennedy, *The Rise and Fall of British Naval Mastery* (London: Ashfield Press, 1986), 276.

Chapter Three

REARMAMENT

Bᴿɪᴛɪsʜ Rᴇᴀʀᴍᴀᴍᴇɴᴛ ɪs ᴜsᴜᴀʟʟʏ ᴅᴀᴛᴇᴅ from the Cabinet decision of February 1936 to lay down five new battleships; create a modernized, five-division army expeditionary force; and build up the Royal Air Force (RAF) to 123 squadrons (1,500 frontline combat aircraft). In fact, as early as November 1933, the Defense Requirements Committee (DRC) had been set up by the Cabinet to survey the damage done by Churchill's Ten Year Rule and MacDonald's defense cuts of 1930–1932. It is wrong to imagine that the British establishment was opposed to Rearmament in principle. They were not. But almost every responsible British official believed that Rearmament had to take place within a framework of free market capitalism and "sound" (i.e., traditional, nineteenth-century) economic policy. As the renowned economic historian Karl Polanyi wrote: "Britain's strategy and foreign policy were constricted by her conservative financial outlook. . . . England's military unpreparedness was mainly the result of her adherence to gold standard economics."[1]

The DRC floundered on arguments over which enemy Britain was arming against. The Treasury considered Germany to be "the ultimate potential enemy." The Navy thought that Japan, which had recently invaded and occupied Manchuria, was the most likely foe. The Foreign Office leaned toward the conclusion that Nazi Germany was the most dangerous threat facing Britain but was still wary of Japan and wanted the Singapore naval base completed to deter her and reassure Australia and New Zealand. The United States had already been written off the list of potential adversaries; almost everyone agreed that America had to be appeased, although some officials, among them Chancellor of the Exchequer Neville Chamberlain, dreamed of a return to the Anglo-Japanese alliance. But, now, an alliance with Japan was seen not as an insurance policy against U.S. aggression (as certain officers at the Admiralty had believed after World War I) but as a means to disengage from Asia and concentrate on Germany. In this atmosphere, it was difficult to formulate any policy that could command a consensus among the political and bureaucratic elite that governed Great Britain. The fact that an election was coming in 1935 made it even tougher. Nevertheless, £50.3 million was allocated above normal expenditures over the coming five-year period to make up for the worst deficiencies in Britain's military forces.[2]

In 1935, Conservative Party leader Stanley Baldwin replaced the ailing Ramsey MacDonald as prime minister in what was still nominally a "National" coalition government. Baldwin, who was nothing if not a shrewd politician, had no intention of running on a platform of Rearmament, for Rearmament would mean increased taxation, cuts in social spending, or a combination of the two. He pledged to the voters that his administration would institute no great armaments program and won in a landslide. Secretly, of course, plans continued to be formulated about how to redress the growing imbalance between the British Empire's limited military might and substantial strategic commitments.

These commitments were extensive. Britain could not allow Germany to dominate the continent of Europe. She had valuable colonies in Hong Kong, Malaya, and Borneo that the Japanese coveted. India was threatened from within by Gandhi and the Congress Party and from without by the Soviet Union. The Middle East was unstable, and trouble was brewing in Palestine. Egypt and the Suez Canal had to be guarded. An eye had to be kept on Fascist Italy in the central basin of the Mediterranean. British trade had to be kept safe from the surface ships and submarines of potential enemies. British cities had to be protected against enemy bombers. The British military in 1935 could not possibly guard against all of these possible threats. Deciding which were Britain's vital interests and what could be bartered away or left effectively defenseless was the issue of the era. It is not surprising that the British never really resolved the problem. In fact, given British resources in money, manpower, and industry, it was insoluble. The chiefs of staff always argued that, alone, Britain was too weak to guard her far-flung empire. She needed more friends, or fewer enemies. But that was the politicians' and the diplomats' job. The primary debate among the military chiefs was over who would get what money that was available and how would it be spent.

Rearmament took place at different rates and under differing sets of assumptions in each of the three branches of the service. This was often for political, rather than strictly strategic, reasons. Yet, separating the political from the strategic rationale for the choices made, or ignoring the personal motivations of the actors involved, would be a mistake. Few actions in life are unalloyed by both the complicated tradeoffs people make within their own psyches and the conflicts between colleagues and coworkers. Britain got the military forces she had in 1939 because certain leading individuals had more clout in government than others and because some people honestly disagreed over whether Germany or Japan was the enemy most likely to strike first. In broadest terms, key officials in the Treasury, along with the Air Ministry and the RAF, were, from 1934, most concerned about Germany. Neville Chamberlain, while at the Treasury and later as prime minister, believed Germany to be Britain's most likely enemy; he thought the German threat best handled by RAF airpower and was against building up the army. On the other hand, the Admiralty wanted to build a fleet to fight the Japanese. The British Army was interested in developing a modern mechanized force to fight the Germans in Europe but was distracted by the need to maintain order within the empire and fears of another bloodbath like the 1914–1918 war. All sides of the argument over Rearmament had good reasons to put forward demands for new weapons and more men; all three services were understaffed and underequipped and lacked the means to carry out successfully even their defensive responsibilities in a future Great Power war. All three services knew that if they could convince the Cabinet that their perceived menace was the most frightening, then they would get the biggest slice of the budget pie. The service ministers (first lord of the Admiralty, secretary of state for war, secretary of state for air) and the chiefs of staff were genuinely concerned about the safety of their country but could not help but be self-serving in arguing that the enemy they wanted to be equipped to fight was the most dangerous, or at least most likely, enemy Britain faced. They could hardly be expected not to make such claims. So, we must look at how each service perceived the threats facing Britain and her empire, what they argued they needed to face the threat, and what, in the end, they were granted by an anxious cabinet in terms of money and resources to meet their needs, real or imagined. Our first stop will be the obvious loser in the interdepartmental battles of the mid-1930s, the British Army.

It was once common to describe the British Army between the wars as hidebound and intellectually moribund. This portrait is misleading. There were deeply conservative elements in the British Army, but they were only one tendency among many. British cavalry officers, often seen as the most conservative element in the army, in fact embraced the tank and wanted all their cavalry regiments mechanized as quickly as money and new technology made it possible. The British Army experimented with tanks and truck-borne infantry working together in mixed formations using radio communication and direct artillery support as early as 1927. British regulations laid down a completely modern combined-arms doctrine in the 1930s, stressing the need for infantry, tanks, and artillery to work together on the battlefield to break the enemy line. Forces of light tanks and mechanized infantry were to exploit battlefield breakthroughs. We know for a fact that German officers followed these developments and incorporated some elements of British thinking in their own blitzkrieg approach. We now also know that British doctrine was undermined by the culture of British command and control.[3]

Since the time of the Duke of Marlborough in the early 1700s, British Army field commanders had led overseas expeditions that were hard for the men in London to control. Communications did not allow for the development of centralized command from back in the capital. So, British field commanders like Marlborough, Howe, Wellington, Kitchener, and Haig had enjoyed a great deal of independent decision-making power. And, unlike the Admiralty, the War Office was not an operational command center. Its job was organizational and administrative. With such great authority vested in field commanders came a terrible tendency to concentrate all critical decision making in the hands of the local general. When he was a genius like Wellington, you did not have a problem. However, most commanders are not Wellington, and modern mobile warfare is too fluid and complex, and modern armies are too big, to be commanded in the iron-fisted manner of Wellington at Waterloo. Therefore, although British doctrine called for a fast-paced style of modern combined-arms combat, British command culture was wedded to an authoritarian model of strict control. Generals may have planned for combined-arms attacks, but the captains and majors out commanding the troops were indoctrinated to obey orders unquestioningly. They lacked a sense of initiative, tended to follow orders rigidly, and failed to exploit opportunities presented to them on the battlefield. Junior and field-grade officers worked to the plan and did not communicate with other local commanders for better coordination or adjust readily to changing conditions. They looked for direction from up the chain of command. This made their actions and reactions ponderous. Many of the more aggressive and nimble-minded young officer candidates gravitated to the RAF and flew Spitfires rather than commanding infantry platoons. The British Army in World War II never consistently achieved the flexibility that the Germans displayed with their looser command style and highly developed sense of teamwork. Additionally, the British Army was loath to expand its pool of perspective officers beyond the well-to-do products of the English boarding schools. Without the large number of college and technical school graduates that Germany and America took for granted, the British turned to their exclusive secondary schools for officer material. Numerically and intellectually, this was too narrow a base to build on. Yet, to gauge the army's attitude, even after Dunkirk, we need only look to a telling comment by the then secretary of state for war, Anthony Eden. When confronted by the fact that the RAF, faced with the daunting task of winning the Battle of Britain, had thrown its doors open to talent, Eden replied: "The officer in the Royal Air Force Squadron is first a technician and a commander only second; the Army officer must be a leader first and a technician second."[4] Obviously, Eden believed that men without a bankroll were not fit to lead.

In terms of size, the British Army was a small, all-volunteer force of highly trained professional soldiers. After the cuts following World War I, the army stabilized at a strength of roughly 200,000 officers and men. In 1928, its manpower was divided into 137 infantry battalions, 23 cavalry regiments, 124 field artillery batteries, 15 light artillery batteries, 6 antiaircraft batteries, 4 heavy artillery batteries, 4 tank battalions, and 11 armored car companies. Of this total, 45 battalions, 65 batteries, and 8 armored car companies garrisoned India.[5] At any given time, about 55 percent of British troops could be found at home and 45 percent deployed throughout the empire. So, British generals could not fail to spend much of their careers either commanding troops in the colonies or thinking about imperial policing. This affected how they viewed the world and the kinds of weapons they thought it important to procure for the army. The British Army thereby suffered from a kind of split personality, conscious of its conflicting colonial and European roles and convinced that it could never get the money or men it needed to perform both duties successfully. This split mission, colonial and Continental, also made the army vulnerable in the bureaucratic battles over funding because the army could not clearly articulate a single message to policymakers explaining what the army would contribute to victory in a future war and how it might accomplish its role economically.

The British Army was assigned its priorities by successive governments in the 1920s and 1930s. Its mission did not significantly change until 1939. First and foremost among its responsibilities, the British Army was to safeguard the empire and ensure its internal peace and cohesion. British Army units during the inter-war years had to perform internal policing operations in Iraq, Egypt, India, China, and, in the late 1930s, Palestine. The deployment to Palestine to maintain order between Arabs and Jews and to suppress an open Palestinian rebellion was substantial. In the summer of 1936, much of the First Infantry Division was deployed from England to Palestine to help maintain order. At its peak, the civil unrest in Palestine sucked in twenty-two British battalions and two cavalry regiments.[6] The suppression of the Palestinian rebellion cost money and prevented these units from training with modern weapons for a conventional war against a modern foe (i.e., Germany).

Second, the British Army was to defend the United Kingdom from invasion. This was a largely theoretical obligation as the navy and air forces would hopefully smash an invasion force before it landed, but it does reveal the insular, defensive thinking of politicians and even army officers during the inter-war period. The army was also responsible for the purchase and manning of the ever-increasing antiaircraft gun defenses of the United Kingdom. So great was this obligation that on December 8, 1937, Chamberlain declared antiaircraft guns to be an "absolute priority" in army rearmament.[7] Two entire Territorial Army (the British equivalent of the U.S. National Guard) divisions were converted to antiaircraft artillery units. By 1938, this added an extra strain to the already tight volunteer manpower pool, and British factories were turning out more antiaircraft guns than either field artillery pieces or antitank guns.

Third, the army was to prepare an expeditionary force for deployment overseas in a time of crisis. Where that expeditionary force was to go—India, Singapore, Egypt, or continental Europe—was much debated. If it were to go out to defend the empire, the Expeditionary Force would have to be highly portable, with light artillery, armored cars, and rugged small arms. If the Expeditionary Force were to fight on the continent of Europe alongside the French and Belgians (presumably to thwart a German invasion of one or both of those countries), it would need tanks, heavy artillery, and lots of trucks. To fight the Germans, it would also have to be much bigger, or at least designed as a cadre force (like the French Army), expandable from a professional nucleus to a mass conscript army in an emergency. The cost-cutting atmosphere of the 1920s made an army designed to fight in Europe impossible because it was uneconomical. The fact that Germany was no military threat in those years clinched the deal. When Hitler came to power in 1933, it became harder to argue that Britain faced no threat from Germany and, therefore, did not need a modern army to fight in Europe. But the needs of colonial policing and the cost of a major modernization delayed efforts to rearm the British Army. The British Army expanded only slightly, despite the introduction of conscription in April 1939, from 197,000 men in 1937 to 224,000 men on September 1, 1939.[8] And much of the money allocated for the British

Army had gone to paying for quality recruits and improving their living conditions, creating new antiaircraft artillery batteries for home defense, and designing new weapons to replace obsolescent ones. The Territorial Army was under strength and poorly equipped. Only two of its twelve divisions were equipped for war in Europe, and the last-minute attempts initiated in April 1939 to double the Territorial Army's strength had not progressed beyond the paper stage when war began in September. The Territorial Army could not speedily reinforce the regular army, and the Territorial Army's rising budget enjoyed an even less flattering place in the hearts of Chamberlain and the Cabinet than that of the regular army. With tight budgets and escalating defense costs, the army was judged to be "low man on the totem pole" and received fewer resources toward Rearmament than the Royal Navy or the RAF. The discrepancy comes into clearer focus when one considers the cost of manpower in an all-volunteer force. The British Army had twice the number of personnel as the Royal Navy and more than three times that of the RAF, so a greater proportion of its budget went to pay and victuals, leaving less money for arms and supplies.

It did not help much that the secretary of state for war (the cabinet minister in charge of the army) from 1937 to January 1940 was Leslie Hore-Belisha. Hore-Belisha was a great advocate for getting rid of the army's horses and immediately replacing them with tanks and trucks. He was anxious about a Continental commitment and wanted a small, elite, highly mechanized army that could help the French but would not be too great a burden on the British taxpayer. He unquestionably stepped on toes. Worse, Hore-Belisha suffered from two awful handicaps: he was a "clever fellow" in a society that did not much like the overtly bright and eager, and he was a Jew in a society that did not much like Jews. He had some good ideas but had trouble instituting them and often acted impulsively. The generals were not inclined to give him a chance, and he lacked the tact and finesse to win them over—not the best of situations with the army fighting for funds and war looming on the horizon.

When war came, the British were in the process of completely converting the army to motorized transportation, the first army in the world to rely totally on trucks and tractors to pull its artillery and carry its equipment. Its 2-pounder antitank gun was the best such purpose-built antitank weapon in service with any army. Many field artillery batteries were being converted to the 25-pounder gun. This artillery piece was the latest development in mobility, accuracy, and rate of sustained fire. The Bren machine gun was reliable and accurate but cursed with a too-small box magazine (thirty rounds), so it could not lay down sustained fire; its users had to aim and fire in short bursts rather than spray an area the way German and American belt-fed machine guns could. Infantry platoons were, however, to be issued the innovative Bren gun carrier, a small tracked armored vehicle. By 1940, only Germany's ten panzer and seven motorized infantry divisions were to be mechanized on the same scale as British infantry divisions; throughout the war, German infantry divisions remained dependent on horses for transport.

British tanks were few in number, and their production was split between three models: a light tank for reconnaissance, a medium cruiser tank for maneuver and the exploitation of breakthroughs, and heavy infantry tanks (the venerable Matilda) for bashing through the enemy front line. British tanks in 1939–1940 were roughly on a par with foreign models but notoriously mechanically unreliable. Lip service was paid to combined-arms operations, but the tanks tended to go it alone on the battlefield.

Despite obvious neglect, much had been done to transform the British Army between 1936 and 1939. New weapons systems were entering production or had already begun reaching the frontline troops. The Bren gun was in wide service, but the 25-pounder had yet to replace the World War I–vintage 18-pounder in many artillery batteries. The 2-pounder antitank gun was in limited service, but many units were forced to rely on the hopeless Boys antitank rifle to stop enemy armor. Doctrine had been developed for fighting a modern war, even if it was undermined by a rigid command culture. If the British Army had a hidden doctrinal weakness, it was in the area of amphibious operation. Little had been done before 1937 to develop the doctrine and equipment needed to land troops successfully against active opposition. The debacle at Gallipoli in 1915, with its appalling losses and indecisive results, had soured the services on amphibious warfare. This aversion was to affect Allied strategic thinking right up to D-day. Yet, the need for a substantial Continental commitment had been acknowledged, and steps were taken to get the army ready to fight the Germans. But when war came, all these efforts proved too little, too late.

The "golden boy" of the 1930s military services was by far the newest, the RAF. Created in 1918, the RAF had gained total control of everything that flew: all of the army's bombers and fighters and all of the navy's attack planes and reconnaissance machines. It was run out of the Air Ministry and had its own cabinet minister, the secretary of state for air. Despite its being a latecomer with the shallowest of institutional roots and the weakest external lobby, the RAF combined the appeal of "high tech" and the promise of a revolution in military affairs. Its prophet, driving force, and first chief of the Air Staff was Marshal of the RAF Lord

Trenchard. Trenchard had climbed the mountaintop and seen the promised land—strategic bombing. No longer would wars be brutal slugging matches as armies trampled the Earth, destroying each other and consuming nations' wealth. In the future, air armadas would strike home on the first day of war, smashing the enemy's industry and his will to keep fighting. Many would die, but the quick results would reduce the overall costs of war in money and lives. Armies and navies were a thing of the past, Trenchard and his acolytes would say at their most bumptious. All you needed was a jolly good air force, and not only would you win the next war (and in record time), but it was almost certain that no next war would ever come, since fear of your bombers would deter any attack. Who would dare risk the wrath of the RAF?

The RAF's share of defense expenditure rose throughout the 1930s, as table 3.1 demonstrates. Last in financial allocations in 1933, the RAF passed the British Army in 1937 and the Royal Navy in 1938. The Treasury particularly favored the RAF; both Neville Chamberlain when he was Chancellor of the Exchequer and the Treasury's permanent secretary, Sir Warren Fisher, believed that Germany was Britain's most likely foe and that the RAF was best suited to

Table 3.1. Annual Expenditures of the Three British Military Services (in millions of pounds)

Year	Army	Navy	Royal Air Force
1933	37.592	53.5	16.78
1934	39.66	56.58	17.63
1935	44.647	64.806	27.496
1936	54.846	81.092	50.134
1937	77.877	101.95	82.29
1938	122.361	127.295	133.8
1939*	88.296	97.96	105.702

*Before September 3.
All figures from Gibbs, *Grand Strategy*, 532.

dealing with her as an enemy. However, Chamberlain and Fisher were not completely sold on the Air Staff's obsession with strategic bombing and wanted fighters and antiaircraft defenses procured as well. Nevertheless, the RAF and its Bomber Command enjoyed a key role in British war planning. Minister for the Coordination of Defense Sir Thomas Inskip argued in 1937 that since the Germans would likely try for a knockout blow against Britain from the air, "the Air Force takes a place second to none in our defense preparations."[9] Chamberlain reiterated this sentiment in talks with the French in 1938; not only was the RAF key to British defense, but it would also be the only Allied force capable of striking at Germany early in a future war. So, no one can say that the British were insufficiently "air minded" in the run-up to World War II. We now have to consider exactly what the Air Staff wanted and what they got.

The RAF hoped to establish and maintain numerical parity with the German Luftwaffe. This was difficult for two reasons. First and foremost, nobody knew the exact strength of the German Air Force, and the Germans were not overly forthcoming on the subject. When Hitler or Hermann Goering made pronouncements on their vaunted strength in the air, they usually lied, overstating German air strength as a deterrent to British or French leaders who might consider launching a preemptive war against Germany. Winston Churchill was famous for repeating these inflated numbers in the House of Commons as a spur to increase British production, but it is not clear that his speeches had the effect Churchill wanted. The government was pretty sure from its intelligence sources that the Luftwaffe was not so large as Hitler claimed, so the Cabinet viewed Churchill's speeches as alarmist. The public was intimidated by the large number of bombers Churchill claimed the Germans already had and were probably made more, not less, cautious about how Britain should conduct her foreign policy out of fear of air attack. So, on a practical level, planning the strength of the RAF based on parity with the Luftwaffe was not easy. Second, how should parity be measured? Should Britain build the same number of bombers as Germany or a different proportion of bombers to fighters than in the Luftwaffe establishment? Could British industry match German industry in aircraft production, and at what cost to navy and army rearmament? These were not minor issues. The British did establish a priority system for their aircraft industry. Advanced aircraft engine design and production had top priority. The speed of an airplane is largely a result of the power of its engine, and the people at Rolls Royce were producing outstanding one thousand plus horsepower engines by 1938. Next in priority came bomber airframes, fighter airframes, attack and reconnaissance aircraft, and, finally, shipboard aircraft for the Royal Navy's carriers. This system was in place by 1937 and was to remain the basic outline of British aircraft production policy until the end of World War II, with the exception of a relatively short period before and during the Battle of Britain in 1940, when fighters commanded top priority.

In late 1937, the Cabinet considered the needs of the RAF, and Chamberlain insisted that fighters for the defense of the United Kingdom receive increased funding. The RAF was already in the process of being expanded from thirty-one thousand officers and men in 1934 to eighty-three thousand on the eve of war.[10] Bombers still predominated in the schemes of the air marshals, but the new, fast monoplane fighters, the Hurricane and the Spitfire, promised a revolution in air defense. The key event for all air forces in the 1930s was the changeover from slow, highly maneuverable

71

biplanes to faster monoplanes powered by a new generation of much more powerful engines. The RAF was in the thick of this transformation. Luckily for the British, the money started pouring into aircraft procurement just as the new designs and engines were ready for production. When coordinated by the Chain Home radar system, Hurricane and Spitfire monoplane fighters would prove a formidable obstacle to German bombers bent on destroying British cities. Radar had been invented in the United Kingdom and first demonstrated successfully in February 1935. By 1936, British radar stations were able to detect planes sixty miles from shore. The Cabinet decided to set up an overlapping chain of radar stations to cover the east coast of Great Britain. Chamberlain and the Cabinet made sure that monies were allocated to build the system and create more frontline fighter squadrons. By September 1939, twenty stations were fully operational and could detect any incoming German bombers hailing from the Continent. This timely expenditure would decide the Battle of Britain and save England in 1940.[11]

Increased fighter strength was all well and good, but how did the RAF stack up against the Luftwaffe? The high costs incurred because of the voluntary nature of British military service, plus large investments in new plant and equipment, made parity with the Luftwaffe a short-term impossibility. The RAF in 1938 was already soaking up the maximum available aircraft production of all British industry. Productive capacity was quickly rising due to government and private-sector investment, but skilled workers then formed a new production bottleneck. In March 1938, it was surmised that British factories could turn out four thousand planes from April 1, 1938, to March 31, 1939. This turned out to be an overestimate. Factories could not keep up with government orders. Eventually, the Cabinet adopted the Air Ministry's "Scheme L," which called for a frontline strength of 608 fighters and 1,320 bombers by March 1939, with an equal compliment of reserve replacement aircraft on hand by March 1940.[12] In aircraft allocation, the British differed fundamentally from the Germans, who always maintained a much greater proportion of their air strength in frontline squadrons and had inadequate reserves of planes and spare parts. The Germans wanted to win their campaigns by means of a knockout blow, whereas the British planned on a long war; therefore, the Germans assigned their aircraft to combat squadrons, whereas the British kept many planes in reserve. An example of the British and German approaches can be seen in statistics for the Battle of Britain. On the eve of the battle (August 10, 1940), the RAF had 749 fighters available with 372 in immediate reserve to replace losses. The Germans had 805 fighters ready for action, but few reserves and even fewer planes leaving the factories. When the battle fizzled out in late September, the British still had 732 fighters fit for service, while the Germans were down to 276 machines. The two sides had lost a similar number of planes, but British reserves of aircraft and spare parts and massive factory production kept RAF Fighter Command well stocked with planes, while the Luftwaffe was bled white.[13] This pattern was equally true in October 1938, when the Luftwaffe had 3,307 frontline aircraft but no reserves![14]

The British had developed two winners in the Spitfire and Hurricane fighters. Each could fly at speeds in excess of three hundred miles per hour, and the Spitfire was as agile as any monoplane then in service. By contrast, contemporary bombers cruised at speeds around two hundred twenty to two hundred fifty miles per hour. Together, the Hurricane and Spitfire were a match for anything that flew in 1939. British bombers, however, left much to be desired. The Whitley, Blenheim, and Hampden were slow, carried a mediocre bomb load, and had few defensive machine guns. They would prove to be sitting ducks in combat against modern German fighters in daylight, completely incapable of carrying out the strategic bombing missions they had been envisioned to fly. Their inadequacies forced the RAF to switch to night area bombing. The next generation of bombers on the drawing boards (the Stirling, Wellington, and Manchester) was a huge improvement over these machines, but they would not take to the skies before 1941.

The impressive performance characteristics of British fighters and the desire to protect the British homeland if war came led to an acceleration in fighter procurement after the Munich crisis of September 1938. That November, it was agreed to purchase an astounding 3,700 fighters by April 1942. Bomber strength was also to be upped from seventy-three squadrons to eighty-five, fully equipped with a new generation of bomber aircraft, all by the same April 1942 deadline. The RAF's budget by this time had risen to first place among the services. Whatever can be said about the Chamberlain government, its commitment to a modern air force and to the air defense of the United Kingdom cannot be doubted. More than any other country, by 1939 the British had made a massive and total commitment of their national resources to air power in all its manifestations. We must now turn to the service that had fought ardently to maintain its claim to be Britain's saber and her bulwark, the Royal Navy.

The Royal Navy was, at least until the mid-1930s, almost universally considered (outside the Air Staff) to be Britain's most essential arm of defense. Only the Royal

Navy could protect England and her imperial possessions from invasion. Only the Royal Navy could project power worldwide. It was still the largest, best trained, and most prestigious navy on Earth (although the navies of America and Japan were very good and getting better). And although the Americans had demanded parity with the Royal Navy, they had never (except in battleships) built up to their tonnage limits under the Washington Naval Treaty. So, the Royal Navy was still the biggest in 1939. The fighting tradition and collective confidence of the Royal Navy made it a formidable force to be reckoned with. But the cost-cutting measures of the 1920s and the limitations imposed by the Washington and London naval treaties had cut into the Royal Navy's fighting muscle. Before we can see how this was true, we have to look at the organization of the Royal Navy and how it was led.

First, an explanation of warship types in the inter-war era is in order. Ships came in several distinct types: battleships, battlecruisers, aircraft carriers, cruisers, and destroyers. Battleships were big, displaced (weighed) about thirty to thirty-five thousand tons, had thick armor protection, and mounted between eight and ten big guns that fired shells ranging from fourteen to sixteen inches across (depending on the ship). They took two to four years to build, were very expensive, and were always in short supply. They were also fairly slow, making from twenty to twenty-three knots (nautical miles per hours). Battlecruisers were as heavy as battleships, often longer (to produce a better hull form and increase speed), and sacrificed thick armor for bigger engines and higher speed. They could make from twenty-seven to thirty-one knots. The Royal Navy had twelve battleships and three battlecruisers after the reductions brought about by the 1930 London naval conference.

Aircraft carriers displaced about twenty to twenty-five thousand tons, had limited armor protection, and acted as floating airfields. Most British carriers could not carry many planes. Existing ships carried between twelve and sixty planes. By comparison, Japanese carriers tended to carry fifty to seventy-two planes and U.S. carriers seventy-two to ninety. The Royal Navy, however, had more carriers than any other power: six in 1938 compared to five American and four Japanese. The Royal Navy planned a major carrier construction program for 1937–1940 involving six new, large, fast ships that substituted heavy armor and antiaircraft guns for a large air compliment; the first three were to carry only thirty-six planes each. This tradeoff was made because the Royal Navy believed the existing generation of carriers in all navies to be extremely vulnerable to attack. They believed that their less vulnerable armored carriers, with their powerful antiaircraft gun batteries, would survive to use their aircraft, while bigger, poorly armored American and Japanese carriers would get sunk. Britain's small remaining air strength would then be perfectly adequate, as its opposition would be lost with the enemy's carriers.

Cruisers could be anywhere from five to ten thousand tons in displacement, with five to twelve 6- or 8-inch guns. They were designed for good sea keeping and endurance and made thirty to thirty-two knots (about thirty-four miles per hour). Cruisers were the "eyes of the fleet" in a time when airplanes were of limited range and often incapable of flying in bad weather. They scouted for the battleships and aircraft carriers, searching the ocean for enemy ships. Although Britain had more cruisers than any other navy, her huge overseas empire and far-flung lines of communications meant that she never had enough.

Destroyers were the smaller cousins of the cruisers. British destroyers usually weighed in at about 1,350 tons, carried four to six 4.7-inch (120mm) guns, as well as deck mounted torpedo tubes, and could make thirty-six knots for short periods. To combat submarines, they carried depth charges and a new underwater echo-sounding device called asdic. Asdic (called sonar in the U.S. Navy) was a British invention that sent electronic "pings" through the water. When the sound wave hit the hull of a submarine, it was reflected back and picked up by the asdic receiver. If you knew how long the ping took to go out and come back and the speed of the signal through water, you could calculate how far away the enemy submarine was. Asdic was believed, at the time, to have initiated a revolution in the detection of enemy submarines, and the Royal Navy put great faith in this invention. They believed that it rendered the submarine much less of a threat than it had been in World War I. Destroyers were maids of all work, protecting the fleet from submarine attack, providing gunfire to knock down enemy planes, and dashing in to launch torpedo attacks against enemy surface ships. Britain built more destroyers between the wars than any other nation, and the British Empire counted 105 modern destroyers (plus about 90 old ones left over from World War I) on hand when war came in 1939.

British naval strategy was built around the execution of two basic missions: the defense of trade and the defense of empire. If Britain was to survive and prosecute a war successfully, she needed to keep her vital trade routes open so that essential supplies could be imported. If the empire was to be protected, enemy seaborne invasion forces had to be intercepted and British reinforcements safely transported to threatened areas. In the 1930s, the empire was most vulnerable to an Italian attack on Egypt and to a Japanese thrust south against Hong Kong, Malaya, British Borneo, and perhaps even Singapore. Of the two threats, the Japanese was considered the greater because of her powerful navy and the great distance that separated the British Empire in Asia and the Commonwealth in the Pacific (Australia, New Zealand) from metropolitan Britain. British naval reinforcements would take weeks to reach the scene, and the Imperial Japanese Navy was bigger, and rated by the Royal Navy as better, than the Italian Navy. So, from the time of the Washington Naval Treaty, serious preparation had gone into developing a naval base at Singapore and planning a hypothetical war with Japan. Admiralty planning called for the dispatch of some or all of the battle-fleet to Singapore, followed by amphibious operations to retake Hong Kong (which was considered indefensible), then a submarine and cruiser blockade of Japan. The rise of Nazi Germany and the deterioration of relations with Fascist Italy eventually called these plans into question. To keep any "Singapore Strategy"[15] viable, the Royal Navy needed a vigorous battleship and aircraft carrier building program. Such a program was initiated in 1936, but the resulting ships would take time to build. Eventually, it became clear that no building program that the United Kingdom could afford would offer simultaneous protection against Italy, Germany, and Japan in a three-front war. For this reason, the chiefs of staff favored a policy of buying off one or more of Britain's potential adversaries; they supported Appeasement.

One man dominated the Royal Navy in the 1930s, Admiral of the Fleet Lord Chatfield. Chatfield was first sea lord (professional head of the Royal Navy) from 1933 to 1938. He had been in the thick of the fighting at the battle of Jutland in 1916 commanding the battlecruiser *Lion*. Chatfield was smart, brave, persuasive, and courtly and could think in the broadest strategic sweeps. As first sea lord, he dominated the Chiefs of Staff Committee and British strategic planning. He was committed to reasserting British naval preeminence and instituted long-term plans for revamping the fleet. For Chatfield, the Royal Navy had to consider Germany, Italy, and Japan all as potential enemies. The nightmare scenario was a war against all three simultaneously. To meet that threat, the navy needed four things: a rebuilt battlefleet; control over its own air force (carrier planes were under RAF control); a steady building program that would encourage industry to invest in new technology, plant, and equipment, as well as supply new ships to the fleet; and first call on Treasury monies over the other two services. He was able to get the first three by 1938, but the RAF won the battle for the largest share of the Rearmament pie. Importantly, his strategic calculations were based on Britain's avoiding war until 1942. He knew that the money and building facilities were just not available in the mid-1930s for a crash shipbuilding program. So, Chatfield became a great supporter of Chamberlain and Appeasement, believing that only by adroit diplomacy could Britain buy the time she needed to put the navy back on a proper war footing.[16] In 1937, he had told the Cabinet (through a chiefs of staff memorandum) that Britain needed a diplomatic initiative to garner additional allies, or to reduce the number of her potential enemies, in order for a viable military strategy to emerge. Gradual rearmament, which would not overstrain the financial sector, was essential because British shipyards and heavy industry needed investment and long lead times to build the modern ships Chatfield wanted and because it was a policy that he could sell to the politicians and that they would buy. In the meantime, until Rearmament had born fruit, Chatfield counseled caution.

Chatfield's greatest battles in the 1930s were bureaucratic. He needed to establish the centrality of the Royal Navy in British defense policy, the primacy of Japan as the most likely enemy, and the right of the navy to run its own air force (the Fleet Air Arm). If the politicians and influential civil servants within government could be convinced that these three assertions were correct, then the navy could get the money it needed. Chatfield tried to get his preferences written in stone using a clear standard by which the strength of the navy could be measured. After World War I, the Royal Navy had been organized around a "one power" standard. That meant the navy was to be maintained at no less than the strength of its nearest rival (i.e., the U.S. Navy). But this standard was insufficient to meet the requirements of sending a fleet to the Pacific in order to beat the Japanese while simultaneously keeping enough naval strength in home waters and the Mediterranean to check any moves by Germany or Italy. Chatfield wanted the Cabinet to establish a new standard saying, in essence, that the navy would get whatever number of ships it needed to match Japan and at least one other major navy; he wanted Britain to go from a one-power standard to a two-power standard. He never got it. Establishing a hard two-power standard would mean that the Cabinet would lose control over naval spending; it would mean that the pace (and cost) of naval construction would be decided in Tokyo, Rome, and Berlin, not London. So, although the Royal Navy was allowed to plan and execute a huge building program in the late 1930s, by far the largest of any power, the Cabinet refused to grant the automatic sanction of a two-power standard. Nevertheless, when war came, the British were building 7 battleships, 5 aircraft carriers, 23 light cruisers, and 31 destroyers. The Royal Navy had in commission 12 battleships, 3 battlecruisers, 15 heavy (8-

inch-gunned) and 49 light cruisers, and 183 destroyers. By contrast, the Germans had 2 battlecruisers, 3 11-inch-gunned pocket battleships (actually very heavy cruisers), 2 8-inch-gunned cruisers, 6 light cruisers, and 22 destroyers commissioned or nearing completion in September 1939. Japan could field approximately 6 battleships, 4 battlecruisers, 4 carriers, 18 heavy and 18 light cruisers, and 104 destroyers ready to pounce at any time if the Royal Navy became overcommitted in European waters. The Italians could throw 4 battleships, 7 heavy and 14 light cruisers, and 49 destroyers into the mix by the spring of 1940. If all three powers acted in concert, only French naval strength could make up the deficit. British maritime superiority was real, but not assured.[17]

It must be kept in mind that, despite its many strengths, serious weaknesses afflicted the fleet. Stores of fuel and ammunition were adequate, but no better. British bombs, torpedoes, and shells, on the whole, were less lethal than those of foreign (especially German and U.S.) navies, largely because of poorer ballistic characteristics and inferior explosives. British ships were, on average, older than German, Italian, and Japanese vessels, with a higher proportion left over from World War I. And unlike the U.S. and Japanese battlefleets, many British capital ships had not been modernized through the replacement of old engines and the installation of new guns, additional armor, and improved fire-control systems during the inter-war period. However, most British battleships were equipped (or quickly being fitted) with radar. The Royal Navy chose to maintain a larger number of smaller carriers than the United States or the Japanese did. British admirals were certain that carrier losses would be heavy and, therefore, that going into battle with two smaller carriers and having one survive to launch its smaller air group was better than risking everything on one big carrier which, when sunk, was of no use at all. The Royal Navy's Fleet Air Arm was losing out in a competitive race with the Americans and the Japanese for large numbers of modern aircraft. Often ignored and starved of funds while part of the RAF, the Fleet Air Arm was returned to the Admiralty in 1937 but took time to disentangle from the RAF. By 1939, it had fallen to third place in terms of strength and effectiveness behind the naval air forces of Japan and the United States. Worse, while Britain was fighting for its life in 1940 and resources were virtually monopolized by RAF Fighter and Bomber Commands, the Japanese and Americans were pouring money and technical know-how into their naval air forces. The Fleet Air Arm would never catch up. So, although the Royal Navy was a large, powerful, and well-led force in 1939 that had thoroughly digested the lessons of World War I and embraced new technology, it had some major weaknesses that were difficult to patch up given the extraordinary strains being placed on the British economy.

The long-term problem in naval rearmament, as Chamberlain and much of the Cabinet saw it, was not the cost of building new ships (though this was, financially speaking, bad enough) but the cost of manning and maintaining them. Chamberlain and others worried that building ships to meet the short-term crisis of German and Japanese aggression was turning into a long-range commitment to endlessly high and constantly rising defense expenditures. The British might safely be able to borrow a large but limited amount of money to build new ships to meet a temporary challenge, but to be forced to endlessly borrow money (or endlessly keep raising taxes) to pay for the upkeep of a bloated defense establishment would, given the arthritic economic growth of the times, ruin the country. Too small a navy would threaten the nation's existence, but too large a navy would bankrupt the country. Finding the middle course between these two unacceptable alternatives was a difficult enterprise that Chamberlain managed quite effectively. And even if the government could have found more money for the Royal Navy, by 1939 bottlenecks in the production of key technical gear (turbines, optical equipment, radar, asdic, guns, gun mountings, armor plate) had brought the fleet building program up against the limits of British industrial capacity. Everything that could be done was being done. Taken as a whole, and unlike the British Army, the Royal Navy was largely prepared for war when it came in 1939.

British politicians have been faulted for being too slow in getting rearmament going in earnest. German rearmament was in full swing by 1935, whereas Britain took until 1937 to gear up to rearm. However, there were mitigating circumstances. The delay can be attributed to three factors: (1) the Conservative Party in power at that time did not want to raise taxes or adopt deficit spending in order to finance Rearmament; (2) Rearmament was initially unpopular and would have hurt the Conservatives at the polls; and (3) events beyond their control were forcing the British to be reactive rather than proactive. We must remember that at no time before 1938 did the British government or the British people want large-scale rearmament. They hoped for negotiated arms-control agreements like the London Naval Treaty of 1930 or arms reductions like those worked out in Washington in 1921–1922. The British were bound to be behind the curve of arms procurement established by the Hitler dictatorship. Hitler took the lead in rearming for domestic and ideological reasons, to jumpstart the German economy, and to militarize and regiment society. The democracies only reluctantly followed. By 1939, Britain was spending over twice the percentage of her gross national product on the military as the United States does in the early 2000s; no one would consider American defense spending a minor financial commitment. So, money was made available to arm against Hitler. Chamberlain was prepared to raise taxes and issue £800 million in special bonds to finance Rearmament. France likewise increased military spending in the 1930s in an attempt to keep pace with Hitler. Both countries had peacetime conscription in place by mid-1939. It would be unreasonable to expect any more from the politicians of that day. The bigger German economy was always a key factor in the arms race, as was the ruthless ability of Hitler to use conscription, confiscation, commands, and coercion to get what he wanted out of his economy. France and Britain were faced with bottlenecks to production in the form of shortages of skilled labor, engineers, draftsmen, machine tools, and scientific instruments. Germany, for historical and cultural reasons, had led both countries in education for decades and probably still does today after losing two world wars. Britain and France were also duplicating each other's efforts; they did not produce one rifle, or fighter, or submarine, but each country produced different types. Being democracies, they could not, at least in peacetime, simply order men to perform certain work or companies to divest themselves of tools and equipment needed for the armaments industries. Plans were put in place to rectify the worst shortfalls, and incentives were granted to industry to help defray the costs of training new workers and buying new equipment, but these things took time. It was this need for time that most affected the military and diplomatic response to the situation.

Most military advisors to the British and French governments during the period from 1936 to 1938 were staunch supporters of Appeasement. For some, fear of war and what they saw as an almost inevitable German victory shaped their judgment about Appeasement. The vast majority of senior officers seem to have believed that Appeasement was necessary to buy time for Rearmament (and the creation of an anti-German alliance system) to reach fruition. They believed that later, in the early 1940s, Allied diplomats would no longer have to take such a conciliatory line toward Germany; in the short run, however, war was better avoided. The man who would have to steer British diplomacy through that most dangerous period, when Germany had the lead and Rearmament had not yet leveled the playing field, would be British prime minister Neville Chamberlain.

Notes

1. Karl Polanyi, *The Great Transformation* (Boston: Beacon Press, 1957), 245–46. Polanyi wrote those words in 1944, which demonstrates that the idea that British leaders were constrained by economics, not merely entranced by a "weak" foreign policy of Appeasement, is not the invention of modern "revisionists."

2. The activities of the DRC are summarized in Keith Neilson, "The Defence Requirements Sub-Committee, British Strategic Foreign Policy, Neville Chamberlain, and the Path to Appeasement," *English Historical Review* CXVIII (June 2003): 651–84.

3. For a brilliant analysis, see David French, *Raising Churchill's Army* (Oxford: Oxford University Press, 2001).

4. Quotation from French, *Raising Churchill's Army*, 73.

5. Anthony Clayton, *The British Empire as a Superpower, 1919–39* (Athens: University of Georgia Press, 1986), 27.

6. Clayton, *British Empire*, 493.

7. N. H. Gibbs, *Grand Strategy*, vol. I (London: Her Majesty's Stationary Office, 1976), 466–68.

8. For 1939, see French, *Raising Churchill's Army*, 63; for 1937, see Gibbs, *Grand Strategy*, 450.

9. Quotation from Gibbs, *Grand Strategy*, 533.

10. Gibbs, *Grand Strategy*, 572.

11. Gibbs, *Grand Strategy*, 594–95.

12. For RAF rearmament in general, see Gibbs, *Grand Strategy*, 565–89.

13. John Ellis, *World War II Databook* (London: Aurum Press, 1993), 232.

14. Ernest R. May, ed., *Knowing One's Enemies: Intelligence Assessment before the Two World Wars* (Princeton, NJ: Princeton University Press, 1984), 258.

15. As Christopher Bell points out in his *The Royal Navy, Seapower and Strategy between the Wars* (Palo Alto, CA: Stanford University Press, 2000), more than one "Singapore Strategy" was developed between the wars to deal with various changing conditions.

16. For Chatfield and the Royal Navy in the 1930s, see Joseph Maiolo, *The Royal Navy and Nazi Germany* (New York: St. Martin's Press, 1998), and Andrew Gordon, *British Seapower and Procurement between the Wars* (Annapolis, MD: Naval Institute Press, 1988).

17. See James Levy, *The Royal Navy's Home Fleet in World War II* (Basingstoke, UK: Palgrave, 2003), 16, chart 1.3.

Chapter Four

1937: CHAMBERLAIN

NEVILLE CHAMBERLAIN LOVED the peace and seclusion of his fishing trips to Scotland. As a boy, he had been equally fond of nature walks and learning the Latin names of insects.[1] As an adult, he preferred to be a homebody, taking dinner with his wife and rarely entertaining or going out to parties. For recreation, he grew orchids and went fishing. The future prime minister was reserved, a bit awkward in social situations, and certainly not prone to idle chat.

Chamberlain revered his father, Joseph, and respected his elder half-brother, Austen, but his closest relationships were with three women: his wife, Annie (whom he married at age forty-one in 1911), and his sisters, Ida and Hilda, to whom he wrote letters regularly. Neville and Annie Chamberlain had two children, a daughter, Dorothy, and a son, Frank. As for his character, Neville Chamberlain was blessed, or cursed, with tenacity and a strong sense of duty. His capacity for hard work was renowned, and his irritation with those who eschewed it profound. Chamberlain had the one great vice of most politicians, egotism, but otherwise led a pretty exemplary life.

Chamberlain and his wife Annie in his days as Chancellor of the Exchequer (courtesy of Hulton-Deutch Collection/CORBIS).

Unlike most British politicians, Chamberlain did not belong to the Church of England. In fact, he was not strictly a Christian, having been raised a Unitarian and then become a skeptic on religious matters later in life. From his early religious training, he seems to have absorbed a progressive, reformist, paternalistic view of society and the obligation of the strong to protect the weak. Neville Chamberlain had certain core beliefs. He believed in the British Empire. He believed in free enterprise. He believed that practical, hard-working men of goodwill could always get the job done. He believed in steady, incremental reform administered by sober, propertied men. He believed in his own ability. He hated war and all forms of social discord. Chamberlain's attitude toward war is well summarized in the adjectives he used to describe its immanence during the crisis over Czechoslovakia in 1938: "How horrible, fantastic, incredible it is that we should be digging trenches and trying on gas masks here because of a quarrel in a faraway country between people of whom we know nothing."[2] The mass slaughter of war was, to him, simply irrational and wrong.

Born in 1869, Chamberlain came from a respectable line of Birmingham manufacturers. The family had made money in the boot business, but his father had started a screw factory and done very well. After prep school at Rugby, he attended the University of Birmingham. He had not planned on a career in politics. He tried his hand unsuccessfully at sisal farming in the Caribbean. Despite several years of backbreaking effort, the farm could not be made to turn a profit, so Neville came home to Birmingham to administer the family's business interests. He took to the job and became a sound, successful financial manager.

Meanwhile, his father, Joseph, and half-brother Austen became huge players in British politics. Joseph was a famed defender of free trade and a staunch enemy of Irish home rule, while Austen was considered a sober observer of policies both domestic and foreign. Both would spend many years in Parliament and serve in various cabinets. So, it was not strange that, in 1915, Neville was named lord mayor of his family's political stronghold, Birmingham, by a respectful city council. He served for a very brief period in London during World War I in Prime Minister David Lloyd George's coalition government, but Lloyd George could not abide him, and he was quickly dismissed. The feisty Welshman could not stand the fastidious Chamberlain. Lurking in the background of the prime minister's antipathy was the fact that Lloyd George represented the radical wing of the Liberal Party, while Neville's father, Joseph, had been the champion of its most reactionary elements, which eventually came to support the Conservatives. This most certainly did not help endear Neville to Lloyd George. The two men developed a passionate hatred for each other. Years later, the wily Lloyd George would get the last laugh in their endless feud. In May of 1940, with support from Chamberlain waning, the aged ex–prime minister would rise in the House of Commons and deliver a spectacular and devastating speech denouncing Chamberlain and demanding his resignation. In less than a week, Chamberlain's government fell.

In 1918, Chamberlain was elected to parliament from Birmingham as a Conservative. Later, he would serve during the 1920s in the Cabinet as secretary of state for health and from 1931 to 1937 as Chancellor of the Exchequer. He did valuable work in reforming local government and increasing access among the poor to health care and hospitalization. His great ambition in public life was to raise the school leaving age from fourteen to fifteen and to improve education. As Chancellor of the Exchequer, Chamberlain was a strict adherent of balanced-budget fiscal orthodoxy, but he did introduce special payments to areas worst hit by the Depression and steered government contracts to firms in depressed areas. He was not well liked but was well respected. Civil servants appreciated his efficiency and the way he handled meetings, avoiding useless chatter and guiding discussions toward well-reasoned decisions. His fellow politicians found him cold, bright, and bossy. He provided what drive he could to Stanley Baldwin's ambling last government. Given his obvious brains and experience, Chamberlain was chosen in May 1937 by the Conservative Party to be the next prime minister of Great Britain and Northern Ireland. He had written of himself to his sister in 1935, "I don't really care much what they say of me now, so long as I am satisfied myself that I am doing what is right."[3] Interestingly, Leo Amery, an enemy of Chamberlain's within the Conservative Party, described him in similar terms: "An autocrat with all the courage of his convictions right or wrong."[4] He could be angry, he could be duplicitous, and he often was pigheaded. Chamberlain was not above spying on his political rivals, especially Winston Churchill, but, of course, Churchill received stolen Air Ministry secret documents and used them to denounce Chamberlain in the House of Commons, so neither could claim the moral high ground in their joint efforts to discredit each other. Deep down, Chamberlain confidently believed he was capable of discerning the right path for Britain to take and was determined that he would stick to it. N. H. Gibbs was not unfair when he wrote of Chamberlain, "His was, in many respects, an inward looking mind. And he found it easy to ignore or to misunderstand the needs of others if those needs ran contrary to his own logic or predilections."[5]

Although his experience was in domestic affairs and finance, Chamberlain had firm opinions on issues of foreign and defense policy. They came out of a coherent worldview. First, the budget must be balanced. Overseas ambitions had to be tempered by fiscal reality. By 1934, Chamberlain had become convinced, with admirable foresight, that Germany, not Japan or Russia, was Britain's most likely opponent in a future war. Therefore, he wanted money to be spent on the armed forces but only on those aspects of the military services that would be most useful in deterring or fighting a future war with Germany. For him, this meant the Royal Air Force (RAF). Chamberlain believed that the RAF could both deter war through the threat of a strategic bombing campaign against German cities and defend Britain in war with fighters that could shoot down German bombers. The menace of attack from the air haunted the inter-war years. People were afraid that whole cities would be laid waste by bombs and poison gas. The Air Staff estimated in 1937 that, in a sixty-day all-out bombing campaign against British cities, the government could expect 1.8 million citizens to be killed or wounded.[6] With professional advice like that, it is hard to blame Chamberlain for wanting to avoid war.

Such visions of Armageddon convinced Chamberlain that war must be avoided through deterrence and diplomacy. He summed up his conception of deterrence (very similar to those developed after the birth of the A-bomb) in a letter to his sister Ida. The point of building up British forces was to make Hitler "realize that it [war] would never be worth while. . . . That is what Winston [Churchill] & Co. never [seem] to realize. You don't need offensive forces sufficient to win a smashing victory. What you want are defensive forces sufficiently strong to make it impossible for the other side to win except at such a cost as to make it not worth while."[7] Like the theorists of mutually assured destruction, Chamberlain surmised that if war was so obviously costly in lives and treasure, all sane men would be forced to avoid it; therefore, it would never happen.

Chamberlain's strategic priorities were clear. First, he wanted a counterbombing force to deter German attack and retaliate if Germany attacked the United Kingdom. He wanted fighters and antiaircraft guns to defend British airspace. His first priority was always the defense of Great Britain. Second, he was prepared to support naval ship construction (within fiscal constraints) in order to protect the empire. Naval building would have the added benefit of supplying the means to defend the sea-lanes of communications on which the British economy depended. Chamberlain fought tooth and nail to prevent any significant expansion or modernization of the British Army. To him, an improved British Army would entail an implied "Continental commitment"; if Britain had a big, powerful army, she would be tempted to send it to the continent of Europe to support Holland, Belgium, or France in a war against Germany. Chamberlain rejected a Continental commitment on two grounds: (1) the huge amounts of money needed to expand and modernize the army would rob the RAF and the Royal Navy of critical, and all too limited, funds; and (2) the dispatch of an army to Europe would mean a repeat of the slaughter on the western front in World War I. For the record, Chamberlain was right on both counts. Britain could not afford and lacked the industrial resources and technically trained cadres to create a first-rate army, navy, and air force simultaneously. He was right, too, about the cost in lives of a Continental commitment. Britain fought longer in World War II than World War I and in more theaters of operations, yet suffered fewer combat casualties. This was largely due to the fact that the British Army was not so heavily engaged against the full weight of the German Army in Belgium and France in 1939–1945 as it had been in 1914–1918. Nevertheless, it may have been impossible strategically for Britain not to raise and deploy a modern army. In 1938, when war with Germany was starting to look unavoidable, Chamberlain was forced to divert greater resources to the army. But he did not want to. The horror of the trenches was ever before his eyes. If he could exclusively lend naval and air support to France, along with money and supplies, he could live with the specter of war. The thought of sending an army to meet the German juggernaut was too terrible to contemplate. Best, he believed, to keep the army a small, professional force garrisoning the empire. If Britain had no modern army, it could not be sent to the Continent. Better to keep things that way.

Chamberlain never opposed Rearmament. The need for enhancing the power of the RAF and Royal Navy was obvious to him. He only demanded that those who supported it be prepared to pay for it. That meant Labour Party hawks would have to accept decreases in social spending, and Conservatives who demanded increases in the military estimates would have to swallow increased taxes. It was easy to stamp your foot in the House of Commons and demand a bigger navy. It was another thing to say how you would pay for it. So, in early 1937, Chamberlain, as Chancellor of the Exchequer, dropped a bomb on his own party. He proposed a new graduated tax on business profits to cover the budget gap engendered by increased military spending. The outcry was huge and immediate. The hypocrisy of his opponents, who wanted more armaments at no cost to themselves, was manifest. Chamberlain had tested those who opposed his policy of Rearmament within a balanced budget. He saw plainly that they were not prepared to put their money where their mouths were. Chamberlain, therefore, felt quite justified in ignoring their council from that point on. He would do things his own way.

Despite his risky challenge to those Conservatives who wanted a rapid increase in military spending, when Baldwin stepped down in May 1937 after the coronation of King

George VI, Chamberlain took his place at Number 10 Downing Street. The graduated tax plan was shelved, replaced by a flat tax on business profits of 5 percent. Unwilling to break with orthodoxy and unbalance the budget, sure that those pushing for unbridled rearmament were paper tigers, Chamberlain set off to find another way to avoid war. Eventually, he was forced to raise the income tax from 25 percent in 1936 to 27.5 percent in 1938[8] and to issue special government bonds to pay for Rearmament, but his basic adherence to the balanced budget remained intact.

Chamberlain thought hard about how he could secure a general diplomatic settlement with Germany and Italy that would ensure peace at a price the British taxpayer was prepared to shoulder. Appeasement of Germany was already the policy of His Majesty's Government when Chamberlain took office. This had more to do with Baldwin's hatred of confrontation than any deep conviction. Besides, the electorate Baldwin understood so well was disinterested in foreign affairs and certainly did not want to pay more taxes. Chamberlain intended to transform the accepted policy of Appeasement from a holding pattern to a dynamic quest for a lasting European peace. But, first, he had to navigate around the most ideologically charged issue of the 1930s, the Spanish Civil War.

The Spanish Civil War was the cause célèbre of its day. It had broken out when disgruntled army officers rebelled against the Spanish government in the summer of 1936. Everyone had an opinion about who held the moral high ground, the left-leaning Republican government or the rebellious right-wing army officer corps. Yet, although almost everyone who was politically conscious in those days took a stand on the Spanish Civil War, it was for that very reason the British and French governments wanted nothing to do with choosing sides. Once it became clear that Fascist Italy and Nazi Germany were backing the rebels and that Soviet Russia was aiding the Republican government, the issue became too hot to handle. Either way the governments in London and Paris jumped, they risked alienating passionate, agitated voters. The democracies opted for what was euphemistically called "nonintervention," which in many polite circles translated to "a plague on both your houses." Britain and France refused to recognize the rebels as a legitimate government but would not send weapons or money to the Republic. In France especially, much pressure was put on the Popular Front government of Leon Blum to help the elected government of Spain fight the Fascist Spanish Army. But Blum knew that if he threw in his lot with the Republicans, he would be inviting angry resistance, perhaps even civil war, among his own citizens. So, as the war in Spain dragged on through 1937 and well into 1938, the ideological divide between those who supported and those who opposed the government in Spain grew more acrimonious. When Italy and Germany sent "volunteers" to fight alongside Francisco Franco's rebel troops, thousands of French, English, and other foreigners made the pilgrimage to Spain to defend the Republic against the Fascists. The fact that many of these people were Communists did not make the Republican cause more popular among Britain's (largely Conservative) elite.

The Spanish Civil War proved a serious distraction throughout the years leading up to World War II and made developing a consensus on how to deal with Germany more difficult. Many people who otherwise disliked Nazism still could not in good conscience act to oppose fascism if that meant an alliance with Soviet-style communism. Others on the Left were sure that Chamberlain and the British establishment were closet supports of the Fascists and, so, did not wish to cooperate with him. Such distrust and division was endemic in the democracies but could be suppressed in Nazi Germany. This made the formulation of German foreign policy, which was exclusively Hitler's prerogative, relatively easy compared to the confusion and compromises that were the hallmark of Anglo-French foreign policy, at least up to the time of Chamberlain's assuming the office of prime minister in May 1937. Whatever his faults, Chamberlain at least knew what he wanted to do (secure a lasting peace) and how he intended to do it (through negotiation and compromise, with a modicum of deterrence thrown in to help make his diplomacy more credible). Political divisions continued, but the drift in British foreign policy that had characterized Ramsey Macdonald's last year in office (1935) and Baldwin's government in 1936–1937 came to an end.

Before we look at Chamberlain's activities as prime minister, a very few words about Chamberlain's chief lieutenants are in order. His foreign secretary was Lord Halifax, a clever aristocratic of even temper and deep Christian convictions. One biographer described him as "the Holy Fox." He opposed the Nazis more strongly than Chamberlain but was temperamentally quite pessimistic and as unhappy about the prospect of war as Chamberlain himself. Sir Samuel Hoare, a Liberal who had joined the National government in 1931 and drifted into the orbit of the Conservatives, was a firm supporter of Appeasement. He became home secretary under Chamberlain. Sir John Simon was made Chancellor of the Exchequer because he could be trusted to toe the orthodox Treasury line and fight for a balanced budget.

Chamberlain had inherited Sir Thomas Inskip as minister for the coordination of defense. (Stanley Baldwin had created this cabinet post in 1936 to do exactly what it promised: coordinate. Churchill and Hoare, among others, had hoped for the job, but Baldwin went with an outsider to military affairs.) Inskip had been attorney general and was considered one of the finest lawyers in England. His job was to adjudicate disputes among the three services, not make military policy. Inskip was to arbitrate between competing service demands and try to make the RAF, army, and navy cooperate. Chamberlain kept him in the Cabinet because he was calm and pragmatic; he could be trusted to work hard in private and to keep his mouth shut in public. Most importantly for Chamberlain, Inskip considered Britain's financial health a "fourth arm of defense"; Inskip believed, as did Chamberlain, that if Britain's economy was damaged and credit ravaged by overspending on too-rapid rearmament, her military forces could never meet the challenge of a future war. Inskip would therefore not clamor for greater defense spending, but he would make sure that every pound allotted to the services was spent wisely.

The greatest foreign policy crisis of 1937 came when Japanese Army officers staged a provocative "incident" at the Marco Polo Bridge near Beijing. China's leader, Chiang Kai-shek, did not help matters, determined as he was to halt the drift of North China into the Japanese orbit. By 1937, the Japanese Army had become a state within the state, completely beyond civilian control and determined to drive both Japanese foreign and domestic policy. Japan had been terribly hard hit by the Depression, and the Japanese Army officer corps fervently believed that only imperial expansion could save Japan from economic ruin and give her the resource base to compete with the other Great Powers. Politicians who stood in the way were assassinated, and constitutional government broke down. So, when the army responded by sending troops to Peking and issuing an ultimatum to the Chinese to withdraw, the government back in Tokyo was not prepared to repudiate its actions. Fighting broke out; both sides were so angry and the situation so tense that it proved impossible to stop it. Japan dove headlong into an invasion of China. The British, who had major trading posts and other concessions in China, ordered their forces in China (an aircraft carrier, five cruisers, seven destroyers, several gunboats, submarines, and smaller ships, plus army battalions at Shanghai and Hong Kong) to protect the lives and property of British nationals but to do nothing to help the Chinese or offend the Japanese. Chamberlain approached President Roosevelt to see if the United States would take joint steps to punish Japan for what looked in London like an unprovoked attack on China or even participate in a naval blockade of the Japanese home islands, but the United States was noncommittal, and the proposals came to nothing. Even after the Japanese sunk the U.S. gunboat *Panay*, Washington refused to consider any collective action with the United Kingdom. Although U.S. Navy and Royal Navy personnel began cooperating in their efforts to guard concessions and evacuate refugees and tentative naval staff talks were held, the crisis passed without Anglo-American action. Chamberlain was convinced by Roosevelt's tough public pronouncements and lack of substantive action that the Americans would bark but were useless when you needed them to bite.[9] Chamberlain's jaundiced view of the Americans, already established by his dealings with them as Chancellor of the Exchequer over issues of debt relief and trade liberalization in the early 1930s, was confirmed. Chamberlain's wariness about the United States was to prove the greatest difference between his and Churchill's approaches to foreign policy and, in the long run, proved much more significant than their differing attitudes toward Appeasement (although the issues were interrelated). Churchill at heart trusted the Americans and believed in the long-term benefits of an Anglo-American partnership, while Chamberlain distrusted America and wanted above all else to protect Britain's independent Great Power status. Churchill could oppose Appeasement because he had faith that the United States would backstop Britain in a pinch. Chamberlain had no such faith and was worried about the cost of American help if it came at all.

Chamberlain's other big headache was France. It was essential to Chamberlain's strategic conception to maintain good relations with France because France had the only army in Europe remotely capable of standing up to Germany's. The only other first-class army belonged to the Soviet Union. But by the summer of 1937, reports were already trickling in through British intelligence that most of the Red Army's top officers were being arrested by Stalin. By the time of the Munich crisis in September 1938, three of the Red Army's five marshals, thirteen out of fifteen of its army commanders, and fifty of its fifty-seven corps commanders had been shot by order of Stalin.[10] The Soviet military was a gutted fish. The British had never been overly impressed by the Red Army; now, in such a state of disarray, the British wrote it off as useless. If Hitler was to be opposed, then the French Army would have to be the linchpin of that opposition. Since Chamberlain would not countenance the creation of a vastly expensive British standing army, he was dependent on that of France. But France was in the hands of a Left-Liberal Popular Front government that the British did not trust. Blum's Popular Front government was ill matched to Britain's Conservatives, and its decision to introduce an eight-hour day for French industrial workers was seen in London as hurting French arms production and sending the wrong message to Hitler. Even worse from the British perspective, by 1937 the French government was faced with a virtually insurmountable strategic dilemma. France was pledged to defend the territorial integrity of Czechoslovakia, Yugoslavia, and Poland, three states created by the Treaty of Versailles from the shards of the Austro-Hungarian, czarist, and German empires. When counting rifles had mattered greatly in the conduct of international diplomacy, France's adding the armed strength of these three states to her side in the early 1920s had made some sense. But with the emergence of motorized armies outfitted with tanks and airplanes, backed by industry and advanced technology, the days when counting rifles was roughly equivalent to counting up potential military power were no more. The Czechs especially were vulnerable to German attack and considered themselves incapable of fending off such aggression alone. The French dared not abandon the Czechs for fear of a stampede of Eastern European nations into the German camp. On the other hand, France's Eastern European allies were now a liability, not an asset. They could not balance out the German military advantage vis-à-vis France. They could, however, drag France into a war she did not want and was not yet prepared to fight. If the Germans chose to march into Eastern Europe, France would likely be forced to fight for allies that were of no strategic value or face national humiliation if her leaders decided to do nothing. French politicians therefore prevaricated wildly; that is, they told everyone what they wanted to hear about their ironclad guarantees while fervently hoping that the Czechs, Poles, and Yugoslavs would never ask for French help in any future confrontation with Germany. Likewise, France maintained a treaty of friendship with the Soviet Union but distrusted Stalin and had no faith that, when push came to shove, the Russians would be of any help in thwarting German aggression. In this strategic climate, war was unthinkable.

The French were as keen as ever to cooperate with Great Britain, but Chamberlain found them difficult to pin down and lacked any deep understanding of French national sensibilities. He would have preferred that the French write off their Eastern European commitments but failed to grasp the blow this would deal to French prestige. The watchword for French policy became containment, trying to keep Hitler bound up in a narrow area of Central Europe. If Hitler wanted Austria, fine; France was not pledged to defend her by any bilateral treaty. But containment and her post-1918 alliance system guided French policy toward Belgium and the states of Eastern Europe and kept alive the French government's desire to reach a modus vivendi with Italy. The policymakers in Paris were hopeful that if they could get all of the major states of Europe to pledge to resist Hitler's aggressive encroachment on their territories, then he would not dare make a move. It was essentially a bluff and could only work if Hitler did not risk too much, too quickly and the major states of Europe stuck together and were all prepared to take collective military action. French policy in 1937 was saved from blowing up in her statesmen's faces by the fact that Hitler was not yet ready to move.

Hitler's move into the Rhineland in 1936 had exposed certain weak points in his dictatorship. First and foremost, the army and the Foreign Ministry had opposed him, at times vociferously. In 1937, Hitler's government was still largely staffed by professional bureaucrats and administrators left over from the Weimar Republic. These people were often quite competent at their jobs and had opinions of their own. Like Stalin, Hitler wanted to rid himself of these experts but was always pulled in two directions on this issue. Stalin simply exterminated the whole bunch in stages from 1928 to 1938. Hitler wanted to remake the government in his Nazi image, but he also wanted to get Germany up and ready to fight a great war as soon as possible. He needed the technocrats, capitalists, and generals if he was going to achieve his "destiny" and win Germany living space and raw materials through military conquest. So, he tried to intimidate, to bribe, to cajole, and to seduce the leading elements in Germany so that they would join him in his crazed campaign for global domination. In many cases, the carrots and sticks of Nazi policy worked, but Hitler was still enraged by any challenge to his untrammeled authority.

Despite this rage at anyone who dared question his judgment, or perhaps because of it, Hitler somewhat mysteriously withdrew from much of the day-to-day operation of government in 1937. He met with his cabinet only five times that year and left his ministers and Nazi party officials to hammer out the details of running the country while he intervened in policy decisions only when he felt compelled to.

Hitler was faced in 1937 with a growing economic crisis he could not dig himself out of. Germany had only marginal gold and hard currency reserves when he came to power. Rearmament did not help the situation as Germany was forced to import key commodities like oil, copper, iron ore, tungsten, and rubber. Hitler tried to solve the problem with import controls, wage and price controls, high taxes, confiscation of Jewish property, and long-term government financing through bonds. Later, Hitler would feast on the gold and currency reserves of Austria and the Czechs, but his economic policy was always hand to mouth and was built on too shaky a foundation to be effective over time. This British intelligence understood, which is why Chamberlain had faith that Germany would soon be forced to moderate her foreign policy, if only to decrease defense spending and prevent a German economic crisis. It also underpinned Allied hopes that, in a long war, Germany would experience economic collapse just as she had in 1918. In practice, however, Hitler's economic policy drove him toward desperation and an even more reckless desire for expansion as a way to loot foreign territory and avert an economic implosion at home. The German Army warned Hitler that his economic house of cards was untenable in February 1937, but he ignored them. Hermann Goering, one of Hitler's ablest lieutenants and the head of his air force (the Luftwaffe) was placed in charge of a new superagency known as the Four Year Plan. This agency was designed ostensibly to wean Germany from dependence on foreign raw materials by creating huge home industries and ersatz, or replacement, products to fill the void in German raw material needs (at least until these raw materials could be captured in the inevitable next war). The Four Year Plan disrupted German economic mobilization for war and produced, at best, mixed results. The program was inevitably short-circuited when war came only two years after its inception, but it kept the ball in the air and bought Hitler a little more time.

What Hitler wanted from his government and his economy was simple: the means to carry out his foreign policy. In 1937, those means had yet to reach fruition. But huge investments in armaments factories and other production facilities were being made regardless of their cost or their long-term economic impact on the nation. These massive expenditures would not bear fruit until the period from 1939 to 1941. In the interim, Hitler's patience was being tested, and it came up wanting. He was worried that his poor health would intervene and that an early death would rob him of his chance to fulfill his destiny. He felt compelled to move against his foes before he was really ready. He would take risks with inadequate means because he was sure he would succeed, for he was not afraid of war, and he believed that every other Great Power was. They would bow to pressure because they did not want to fight. He would risk a fight even if he did not have the means on hand to win one. What Hitler did have was an unshakeable will and confidence in his mission. What he lacked in the way of modern arms, his enemies lacked, too. After his 1937 lull, Hitler's time of waiting was just about over. Since the occupation of the Rhineland, Hitler had talked in public of nothing but peace, but a pronouncement in November 1937 would prove portentous: "I am convinced that the most difficult part of the preparatory work has already been achieved. . . . Today we are faced with new tasks, for the Lebensraum [living space] of our people is too narrow."[11] Chamberlain could hardly have imagined what was coming.

NOTES

1. David Dilks, *Neville Chamberlain*, vol. I (London: Cambridge University Press, 1984), 23.

2. Quotation from Ernest May, *Strange Victory* (New York: Hill and Wang, 2000), 165.

3. Quotation from Graham Stewart, *Burying Caesar: The Churchill-Chamberlain Rivalry* (Woodstock, NY: Overlook Press, 2001), 274.

4. Quotation from Ernest May, *Strange Victory*, 172.

5. N. H. Gibbs, *Grand Strategy*, vol. I (London: Her Majesty's Stationary Office, 1976), 510.

6. Stephen Roskill, *Naval Policy between the Wars*, vol. 2 (London: Collins, 1976), 335.

7. Stewart, *Burying Caesar*, 387.

8. G. C. Peden, *British Rearmament and the Treasury* (Edinburgh: Scottish Academic Press, 1976), appendix IV.

9. B. J. C. McKercher, *Transition of Power* (Cambridge: Cambridge University Press, 1999), 240–47.

10. Alan Bullock, *Hitler and Stalin: Parallel Lives* (New York: Vintage, 1991), 489.

11. Bullock, *Hitler and Stalin*, 455.

Chapter Five

1938: MUNICH

British Rearmament was in full swing by 1938, but Germany's larger economy and Hitler's monomaniacal effort to rearm quickly had created a window of opportunity for Germany to exploit her expansionist aspirations. The Royal Air Force (RAF) would be ready to face Germany's Luftwaffe in 1940 or 1941; the Royal Navy's building program would be largely completed in 1942. The British Army's Continental commitment had been rejected in 1937 and, therefore, was not considered a factor. What British policymakers feared were aggressive German thrusts in 1938 or 1939, too early for Britain to parry successfully. They did not have long to wait for their fears to be realized.

By the winter of 1938, it was clear that Italy was realigning diplomatically toward Germany. Italy had fought against Germany in World War I and sent troops to the Brenner Pass in 1934 in support of France when Hitler looked like he would annex Austria. But the split between Italy and the Anglo-French over Ethiopia and open Italian support for Franco and his Spanish Fascists had led Benito Mussolini to drift into Hitler's orbit. The fact that, in 1938,

Hitler could count on Italian support, while Britain and France could not, would bolster the German führer's courage and undermine that of the British and French.

The year began with German rumblings toward Austria. Hitler had long dreamed of uniting all ethnic Germans into a greater Germany. The anxious climate induced the British Cabinet, on February 22, to approve aircraft production to the limit of Britain's industrial capacity. The French were concerned but had no plans to fight if Austria was invaded. Neither did the British. On February 12, Hitler, at a meeting in his Alpine retreat, the Berghof, browbeat the Austrian chancellor into signing an agreement that placed Austrian Nazis in key government posts and released all Nazi Party members from Austrian jails, even those convicted of violent crimes. Austrian prime minister Schuschnigg tried to abrogate the agreement once he got back home by calling for a vote of the Austrian people: did they want to join Nazi Germany or not? Enraged Austrian Nazis, following directives from Germany, took to the streets. Schuschnigg eventually resigned, and German troops entered Austria on March 12. At a critical moment, Hitler got Mussolini's assurance that he would not support any Allied move to stop the annexation of Austria. Not a shot was fired in defense of Austrian independence. On the contrary, wildly cheering crowds met the Germans, and Hitler returned to the land of his birth in triumph. He announced that the plebiscite over Austrian incorporation into the Third Reich would proceed and campaigned in front of ecstatic throngs in Vienna and Linz. The British and French were angered, but newsreel footage of delirious Austrians made thoughts of war ridiculous. If the Austrians were not going to fight and die for their country, why should Englishmen and Frenchmen? German speakers in Austria and Germany were now members of one country. Hitler's restive eye cast about for other German populations to "liberate."

The demise of Austria meant that German troops could now strike at France's ally, Czechoslovakia, from the southwest as well as the north. Many Czech defensive works were outflanked by the German position in Austria. This did not bother the British much as they wanted France to disentangle herself from her alliance system in Eastern Europe and to concentrate on what mattered to Britain—keeping Belgium and Holland out of German hands. But the French were not yet quite prepared to write the Czechs off. They hoped that Czechoslovakia's alliance with France would spell "keep off the grass" to Hitler and that the Nazi leader would leave well enough alone. They were disappointed.

Within the borders of Czechoslovakia lived a large, restive community of ethnic Germans. They made up 22 percent of the total Czechoslovakian population and lived primarily in the Sudeten mountains, the Sudetenland. Their leader, Conrad Heinlein, was a Nazi sympathizer in the pay of German intelligence. Hitler instructed Heinlein in late March 1938 to begin a campaign of violence and agitation designed to destabilize the Czech regime. Hitler's clear motive in all of this was to use the Sudeten Germans as a Trojan horse. He wanted Heinlein to make impossible demands on the Czech government so that the Czechs would be forced to suppress the Sudeten Germans and give Hitler an excuse to intervene militarily on their behalf. On April 21, he ordered his generals to begin planning a lightning strike on Czechoslovakia. Hitler figured that the Czechs lacked the will to resist, the British and French would not want to fight, and Russia, without a border with Czechoslovakia or Germany at that time, could not or would not act. Hitler neutralized the Hungarians and the Poles by dangling before their covetous eyes the promise of valuable border areas of Czechoslovakia if they acquiesced to his plans. All Hitler had to do now was manufacture a crisis and push until his divided enemies capitulated to his will.[1]

Heinlein carried out his mission well. He demanded virtual independence for the Sudeten Germans. Terrorist violence made the Czech authorities look feeble, and the British and the French both urged the Czechs to concede in order not to give Hitler an excuse to invade. One problem often overlooked by later historians was that nobody really believed (except the Czechs) in the inviolability of Czechoslovakia's borders. Czechoslovakia was less than twenty years old and had been cobbled together at Versailles out of parts of the old Austro-Hungarian Empire. The fact that Czechoslovakia's German minority might wish to depart and join up with Germany was a surprise to no one. The fact that Hitler might well try to exploit this was also understood at the time. Once the Versailles Treaty and the League of Nations enshrined the principle of national self-determination as legitimate grounds for a people to decide their own political destiny, it was tough to argue that ethnic Germans had no right to join other Germans in one sovereign German nation-state. Also, the Slovaks were not thrilled with the political makeup of Czechoslovakia either and would later opt for independence, first under Hitler's tutelage and again in the 1990s after the collapse of the Soviet bloc. Hitler held all of the rhetorical and diplomatic cards and played his hand quite well.

Hitler, however, faced opposition at home. The German Army was all too aware of the extent to which Hitler was bluffing. Germany was in no shape to fight a major war—yet. Like their British and French counterparts, German generals urged caution. They might guess that the British and French

Europe's last chance to settle her disputes peacefully: The Munich Conference, September 1938. From left to right Herman Goering (in white uniform), Chamberlain, Benito Mussolini, Hitler's translator, Hitler, and Edouard Daladier (courtesy of CORBIS).

were not ready either, but they knew without a doubt that German stocks of ammunition, trained manpower, and modern tanks and planes were not adequate to the task of annihilating the Czechs quickly, much less winning a world war. And we must not forget that Germany had lost World War I to the very British and French forces they would now have to fight again. For Germany's military leaders, a new war was a dangerous uncertainty. Historians today know that Britain and France did not match up well against Germany in 1940; what historians of today sometimes forget is that Britain and France had been more than capable of halting the Germans in 1914. While we can read history backward and predict an easy victory in 1940, the Germans in 1938 could not. German generals could remember the battle of the Marne and the collapse of their army in November 1918; they were not too keen to start another war. The German generals did not understand that Hitler's calculations were largely political. Hitler believed that he would triumph through the power of his will and the weakness of his enemies, short of actual war. Given their uncertainties as to the outcome of the impending war, a small group of German officers began clandestine communications with the British, urging them to stand up to Hitler so that they could overthrow him in a coup. Chamberlain himself learned of this and thought the whole thing a trap, a disinformation campaign launched by German intelligence to force Britain into a war. He was wrong but understandably cautious. Just how likely it was that a small clique of German officers would have been able to overthrow the Nazi state is tough to imagine. The sad fact is that the German generals did not move, and for a short time, Nazism thrived. It is unlikely that they could have succeeded, but they might have bought the Allies additional time as Hitler got his house back in order. They certainly would have saved their personal honor. Nevertheless, General Ludwig Beck, the chief of the General Staff, resigned over the Czech crisis. Even before Munich, General von Blomberg, the German minister of defense, had been dismissed earlier in 1938 and his post dissolved. In 1938, Hitler also got rid of the commander in chief of the German Army, General Baron von Fritsch, on trumped-up charges of homosexual activity and fired the foreign minister, Baron von Neurath. All who claimed to have a vision independent of Hitler and his Nazi Party were now out of the way. The German Army had lost its traditional right to advise the government on policy and strategy. Under Hitler, it was to be responsible exclusively for handling the technical problems of realizing Hitler's will. Hitler's authority was, by September 1938, untrammeled by the old German elites. Hitler would determine all policy and make all critical decisions.

In April, the Popular Front government of French premier Leon Blum fell. It was replaced by a Center-Right government under Edouard Daladier. Daladier was a capable politician and was well known in European political circles. With some behind-the-scenes prodding from the British, Daladier agreed to appoint Georges Bonnet as his foreign minister. Bonnet had only one overwhelming policy goal— to avoid war. Bonnet wanted to concentrate on Anglo-French cooperation and, if possible, to dump the Czechs. Daladier was ambivalent about his future course of action and summed up his dilemma in a letter to Chamberlain: "France is governed by two equally powerful feelings: the strong desire not to have to fulfill its obligations [to the Czechs], but also the determination to act honorably if Germany forces its hand."[2] French statesmen could not see any way out of this bind, and the contradiction paralyzed their policy until they were swept up in the Munich crisis and forced to face facts; they either had to accept an all-out war with Germany or abandon the Czechs. However hard they looked for room to maneuver, they never found any, and Hitler was not interested in giving them some. France's only escape lay in negotiations or German inaction, but Hitler was prepared to act, and, for him, Czechoslovakia's continued existence had become nonnegotiable.

Throughout the summer of 1938, German workers dug ditches and poured concrete along the border with France. Hitler wanted a defensive belt, a West Wall, completed without delay. He brushed aside the admonition of his field commander, General Adam, that the defenses were not even close to being ready; if the French marched, Hitler was told, they could not be held in check for long. Such practical considerations were immaterial to Hitler. He needed the psychological security that the West Wall offered him and a public show that his intentions were defensive, not aggressive. Of course, the West Wall was being built to cover Hitler's rear so that he could move against his perceived enemies in the East. But the Western Allies and the German people needed to be reassured in the meantime that Germany had no intention of breaching the peace. The lull would make the psychological shock when Hitler decided to act that much more effective.

Chamberlain saw the writing on the wall after Austria was absorbed into the Reich. Czechoslovakia would likely be next. Hitler wanted the Sudetenland, and to avoid war, Chamberlain meant him to get it. In July, he sent Lord Runciman to Prague to act as a mediator between Edvard Beneš, the Czech president, and Heinlein, head of the Sudeten Germans. Neither side had any interest in compromise. As the summer waned, it looked as if war might be in the offing. Nobody but Hitler wanted it, and that was his great advantage. The standoff inside Czechoslovakia left all of the statesmen of Europe staring down the barrel of another world war before the end of 1938.

Chamberlain and Daladier had sound strategic reasons for avoiding war in 1938. The British Army could never match the German Army in numbers or equipment, even if successive British governments were prepared to lavish large sums of money on it, which they were not. British military intelligence estimated that the German Army contained forty-three infantry divisions, three panzer divisions, one mountain and one light division, and a cavalry brigade, plus twenty-one to twenty-four *Landwehr* (National Guard–type) divisions. In all, they estimated the Germans could mobilize seventy-four divisions. In actuality, the Germans had the potential to mobilize seventy-five divisions.[3] In contrast, the British Army could send two divisions to support the French and another two some weeks later. The Czechs could potentially field thirty-four divisions.

The Royal Navy had only just laid down a powerful armada that would not be ready for at least two years. Of those ships in commission, two battleships and a battlecruiser were in dockyard hands being modernized and would not be available for action until well into 1939 at the earliest. The RAF had yet to reach parity with the Luftwaffe. Although orders for new planes were pouring out of the Air Ministry, only four squadrons of the new Hurricane monoplane fighters were operational in September 1938, and the Chain Home radar system was not completed. The French Army's structure and doctrine precluded a swift offensive that might aid the Czechs before they succumbed to a German invasion. The commander in chief of the French Army, General Gamelin, was not sanguine about French chances in a war, and the French Air Force was explicitly dire in its predictions about the outcome of a contest with the Luftwaffe. A top French Air Force officer went so far as to tell the air minister, "I am quite convinced that if a conflict erupts this year [1938], the French air force would be wiped out in a few days."[4] Russia was seen as unreliable and undesirable as an ally and as largely toothless due to the Great Purge. Italy was a wild card but likely to throw in its lot with the Germans. Japan had already demonstrated amply her aggressive intentions in China. The United States was unshakably isolationist. It is true that the Germans were not ready for war either, but the Allies were not sure how unready, and everything in warfare is relative. A mediocre army can very often beat a bad army. Conflict is not measured against abstract absolutes of excellence or ineptitude. It is a contest between whatever forces show up on the day of battle. The British and French knew their own weaknesses, which were many, and fixated on them. Their military leaders were unsure about the outcome of a war with Germany, so they continued to advise their governments to avoid one. Intelligence reports reaching both London and Paris indicated that the German military was preparing for war with Czechoslovakia. German military potential was slightly overestimated, especially the speed at which reserve formations could be brought up to war footing, but, overall, the Allies had a fair idea of what they were up against. The Allied military leaders did not wish to expose their weaknesses in a premature war but to work toward their elimination. All of these considerations factored heavily into the calculations of the British and the French as the Munich crisis hit its stride.

Chamberlain had concluded by the time of the Munich Conference that he would not fight to maintain the territorial integrity of Czechoslovakia. That fact must be kept in mind before we explore the details of the crisis created by Hitler's desire to annex the Sudetenland. We cannot forget here what Cambridge historian T. C. W. Blanning has called "the obvious but often-ignored fact that a state cannot go to war all by itself, that it takes 'two to tango.'"[5] Chamberlain was determined to refuse Hitler's invitation to the dance. He wanted to negotiate a rational compromise solution that retained the Czech state yet met the demands of the Sudeten Germans. Above saving face or preserving the Czech state, Chamberlain wanted to keep the peace. The French just wanted the nightmare confrontation to be over one way or another. These were the inescapable facts that have to be remembered, or the course of the crisis will baffle the reader. Once we understand what the protagonists wanted, the way it all played out makes more sense.

On September 4, Beneš caved into Heinlein's demands at the urging of the British and French. It was not enough.

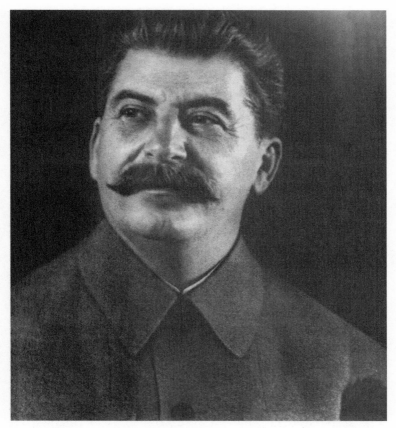

On the sidelines, anxiously awaiting a suitor who would pay his price: Soviet dictator Joseph Stalin (courtesy of The Library of Congress).

Hitler told Heinlein to make new, even more unrealistic demands. Then, on the September 13, the Sudeten Germans attempted a revolt against the Czech authorities. It was put down within hours, but British intelligence warned Chamberlain that Germany might strike at any time. Chamberlain tried a desperate gambit. He informed Hitler that he wanted a face-to-face meeting with him in Germany as soon as it could be arranged. On September 15, Chamberlain took the unprecedented step of flying to Germany to meet Hitler at a mountain villa outside Berchtesgaden. There, Hitler and Chamberlain agreed to a partition of Czechoslovakia, to be carried out district by district in a series of local votes. The people of each area would vote on whether or not they wished to be incorporated into Germany or remain under Czech authority. The Versailles Treaty had set a precedent for such a plan. After World War I, Silesia and the Saar had been allowed to vote on their status. Why not give the Sudeten Germans the same opportunity?

Chamberlain flew back to England and informed the Cabinet of the deal on the table. The French were belatedly consulted and insisted that the agreement include a clause guaranteeing the territorial integrity of the reduced Czech state. Aside from that one condition, both powers agreed that the Czechs should and must agree to Hitler's terms as Chamberlain had negotiated them. The Czechs came onboard as they felt they had no choice. The Soviets made some squeaks in the East but also made it quite clear that they would not go to war over Czechoslovakia unless France did first. The Czechs lacked the will to fight alone and dared the other powers to stand by while Hitler annihilated them. The scene seemed set for a compromise to Germany's advantage. Chamberlain flew to the German resort town of Bad Godesberg on September 22 to meet with Hitler and finalize the deal.

What he discovered when he got there was a Hitler in no mood to compromise. He wanted war. Chamberlain's neat and legal plan was cast aside. Hitler demanded that the votes take place only after German troops had occupied all of the disputed territories. He further demanded that the Czechs accept a German occupation of the Sudetenland immediately. Chamberlain was angered by the changes and got into a heated discussion with Hitler, but the result could not have been in doubt. The meeting broke up with no agreement. Chamberlain flew back to London, where he faced a divided Cabinet. He had been completely bamboozled at Bad Godesberg. Chamberlain was incapable of penetrating Hitler's irrationality and refused to face the fact that Hitler was not negotiating—Chamberlain was being dictated to. However, Chamberlain did grasp the crux of the matter: the choice was between concessions or war. Some in his cabinet wanted to resist Nazi aggression. Others were unsure. Chamberlain believed that war would be a catastrophe and that nothing could be done to save the Czechs. The government ordered trenches dug in London parks and gas masks distributed to regional centers in case war broke out. Chamberlain ordered the Royal Navy's Home Fleet mobilized and dispatched to its war station at Scapa Flow in the Orkney Islands. War seemed inevitable, despite pleas for restraint from President Roosevelt in Washington, D.C. Europe had reached the brink.

In desperation, Chamberlain appealed to Mussolini to mediate the dispute as he was not at that time formally allied to any of the nations involved. On September 28, while speaking in the House of Commons, the message relaying Mussolini's reply arrived. In it, Mussolini stated that he had convinced Hitler to convene a conference in Munich at which Britain, France, Germany, and Italy would decide the fate of Czechoslovakia. When Chamberlain read Mussolini's message aloud, hundreds of members of Parliament rose to their feet and cheered. War might be averted after all.

On September 29, 1938, Chamberlain flew to Munich. Hitler refused to include the Czechs in the negotiations, saying that if the issue was one between Germany and Czechoslovakia only, then he would settle the matter directly with the Czechs. Since the British and French knew this meant war, they preferred a Great Power summit. The details are of little importance as the outcome was inevitable. The British and French tried to negotiate, but they could only capitulate. They agreed to Hitler's demand for an immediate German occupation of the Sudetenland and then informed the Czechs of the details. Britain and France had at no time made any serious efforts to coordinate their diplomatic positions. Both knew that any such effort would be futile anyway as they could not bargain effectively unless they were prepared to fight, and neither country was. They might have bluffed, but they feared that an irate Hitler might just cancel the summit and invade Czechoslovakia. The Czechs themselves chose not to fight alone and submitted to their fate rather meekly (by contrast, when faced with as grim a choice, the Norwegians chose to fight and did so valiantly from April to June 1940). German troops marched into the Sudetenland on October 1. The crisis was resolved, the Czech majority was (temporarily) saved from Nazi occupation, and war was averted.

The morning after the general consensus was reached, Britain, France, Germany, and Italy signed the Munich Agreements. Chamberlain met Hitler and presented him with an additional joint declaration for both of their signatures. It read,

> We regard the agreement signed last night and the Anglo-German Naval Agreement as symbolic of the desire of our two peoples never to go to war with one another again.

> We are resolved that the method of consultation shall be the method adopted to deal with any other questions that may concern our two countries.[6]

Hitler promptly signed. With this piece of paper, Chamberlain flew home to a hero's welcome. Crowds met his plane at Hendon airport and cheered his accomplishment. From his window at Number 10 Downing Street, Chamberlain told the assembled crowd below that the agreement was the harbinger of better days: "I believe it is peace for our time."[7] Newspapers heralded this deliverance from war. Although some in Parliament would lament being seen as having capitulated to Nazi demands, almost all were glad that war had been averted. Although support for the Munich Agreements was not universal, their appeal was broad and deep. Chamberlain enjoyed a 57 percent approval rating in October 1938, a 59 percent approval rating in April 1939, and a 65 percent approval rating in September 1939, when war broke out.[8] These are high marks given the class divides and deep political loyalties common in Great Britain. Yet, Duff Cooper, the first lord of the Admiralty, resigned in protest over Munich, and a few other leading Conservatives, like Anthony Eden, Leo Amery, and Winston Churchill, denounced the agreement. The Labour Party was uneasy but lacked a coherent alternative to Chamberlain's policy. The price of Munich soon became clear, and as it did, the humiliation rankled. A new national consensus began to emerge that no such concessions could in the future be tolerated.

Daladier returned to France and was quickly greeted with a list of demands from his service chiefs for increased military spending. General Gamelin was convinced that Munich had done nothing to lessen the likelihood of war. He and the heads of the navy and the air force had an expensive list of weapons and supplies they deemed essential if, or more likely when, the showdown with Germany erupted. Daladier was chastened by the cost but, nonetheless, did his best to give the military what it wanted. He was able to get an ideologically divided French parliament to go along with the tax increases and social-spending cuts such huge hikes in military spending demanded. The cost of delay was seen as unacceptable. France would have to be ready to fight, and soon.[9]

In hindsight, it cannot be denied that Munich was a diplomatic fiasco. Its popularity at the time is understandable, but that does not change the fact that the Allies were pushed around and the Czechs rolled over and played dead. But was it a failure? No. In practice, the British and French lacked the will, the public support, the weapons, and the doctrine to beat Nazi Germany in 1938. They lacked credible allies; even Canada, South Africa, and Australia were unlikely to support Britain in a war over Czechoslovakia. The Americans were worthless in these circumstances, and the Russians probably were also. The lateness in the campaigning season and the needs of mobilization precluded any serious Anglo-French operations until the spring of 1939. As for the Czechs, they have been credited with having a fine army and good equipment and fortifications, but they folded like a cheap tent in a hurricane. Would the Czechs have held out that long? The much stronger Poles were defeated in less than a month in 1939. Why would anyone think that the Czechs would have faired better? Those who chastise the British and French for not intervening in September 1938 predicate their argument on the assumption that the Czechs would have put up a creditable defense of their homeland. The Czechs showed no inclination for doing any such thing. And if the Czechs proved unprepared to die themselves for their country, why should British and French troops have died for the Sudetenland?

In the end, for Chamberlain, the issue came down to a new world war or the Sudetenland to Germany. He chose the latter. Rearmament had not yet rectified the deficiencies in British military strength. The French were not inclined to act. The Soviets were unreliable. Germany looked stronger than she actually was, but the British could only speculate about what Hitler really had up his sleeve. Chamberlain knew for certain that he could not protect British cities from the rain of bombs and gas that everyone thought would come with the declaration of war. Chamberlain believed that by conceding the Sudetenland, he had prevented war and finally gotten Hitler's signature on an agreement that solved the worst problem of the age. The peace that Versailles had only hinted at could now be real. Consultation would take the place of confrontation. Germany had been granted all reasonable and legitimate concessions. Virtually all ethnic Germans now resided within the confines of the German nation-state. The crisis period before Rearmament had been weathered. If Hitler had any sense, then the two agreements signed at Munich would surely be the dawn of "peace for our time." But this was not to be.

Hitler very quickly grew disillusioned with the Munich Agreements. He became angry that Mussolini and Chamberlain had pushed him from his course toward war and into multilateral negotiations. In 1945, dictating his political testament to his secretary in the bunker beneath the ruins of Berlin, Hitler stated, "We ought to have gone to war in 1938. Although we were ourselves not fully prepared, we were better prepared than the enemy. September 1938 would have been the most favorable date."[10] True or false, Hitler convinced himself very soon after Munich that the remaining rump state of Czechoslovakia had to be destroyed. He saw it as an affront to his pride and a reminder that he had not gotten all he had wanted at Munich. He was also sure that no accommodation could be reached with Britain that would satisfy him. In January 1939, the German Navy was granted top priority in the procurement of steel and skilled workers. Hitler would need a large navy if he were going to settle matters with the meddlesome Chamberlain. As the New Year began, a fuming führer, still unsatisfied with his accomplishments, considered his next move.

NOTES

1. Alan Bullock, *Hitler and Stalin: Parallel Lives* (New York: Vintage, 1991), 562–65.

2. Quotation from Robert J. Young, *In Command of France: French Foreign Policy and Military Planning, 1933–1940* (Cambridge, MA: Harvard University Press, 1978), 203.

3. Ernest R. May, ed., *Knowing One's Enemies: Intelligence Assessment before the Two World Wars* (Princeton, NJ: Princeton University Press, 1984), 253.

4. Quotation from Young, *In Command of France*, 198.

5. T. C. W. Blanning, *The Origins of the French Revolutionary Wars* (New York: Longman, 1986), 210.

6. A. J. P. Taylor, *English History: 1914–1945* (Oxford: Oxford University Press, 1965), 429.

7. Taylor, *English History*, 430.

8. G. A. H. Gordon, *British Seapower and Procurement between the Wars* (Annapolis, MD: Naval Institute Press, 1988), 171n73.

9. Ernest May, *Strange Victory* (New York: Hill and Wang, 2000), 181–84.

10. Bullock, *Hitler and Stalin*, 583.

Chapter Six

1939: TO WAR

THE BRITISH SUFFERED from a jittery hangover following the Munich celebrations. Men like Anthony Eden, Duff Cooper, and Winston Churchill never tired in their efforts to shame the population for embracing the climbdown from war, and even those who had supported the Munich settlement were uneasy about having suffered what could only be seen in the glare of twenty-twenty hindsight as a diplomatic defeat. In the future, Hitler's demands might not allow for any kind of acceptable diplomatic settlement; war was in the air.

Already, in November of 1938, the true ugliness of the Nazi regime was exposed in the pogrom known today as *Kristallnacht*, the night of broken glass. A young Jewish refugee had shot a German diplomat in Paris. Enraged gangs of Nazi Party storm troopers took to the streets of Germany, burning synagogues, smashing and looting Jewish shops, and attacking Jews wherever they could lay hands on them in imagined retaliation for this "racial" insult. The concentration camps, which had originally been built to house political prisoners, began to fill with Jews. A surprising number of Germans were disturbed by the lawlessness, and it was quickly suppressed, but the raw savagery of Nazi anti-Semitism had been laid bare. Many abroad, who had seen German demands for a redress of Versailles-related grievances as legitimate, were no longer sympathetic to a government that would condone such brutality.

"1939 will be a critical year, as it is most unlikely that Hitler will not have some great scheme he wants to put through."[1] So wrote Admiral Sir Roger Backhouse (who replaced Lord Chatfield as first sea lord in 1938) to his Mediterranean Fleet commander. In January 1939, reports reached the British that Hitler intended to invade Holland. Consternation reigned. We now know that these warnings were being issued clandestinely to British intelligence by anti-Nazi officers in German intelligence anxious to prod the British toward action against Hitler. The reaction in London did cause a shift in British policy. Admiral Backhouse used the crisis as an opportunity to push for a startling change in British imperial strategy. He wanted to launch an immediate offensive in the Mediterranean against Italy once war with Germany (and presumably Italy) broke out. This would mean that no fleet would be available to go out east to Singapore to deter Japanese aggression and cover Australia and New Zealand. Lord Chatfield, now minister for the coordination of defense, was horrified. Committing the entire fleet to a war in Europe would leave Britain's Asian empire and Pacific dominions wide open to attack. Nevertheless, Chamberlain (and later Churchill) would be seduced by the idea of gaining a quick victory over Hitler's ally, Italy. The argument for a Mediterranean strategy gained ground quickly because it was believed that an attack on Italy would force Germany to divert resources from the main front in France and the Low Countries and might knock Italy right out of the war. In addition, an attack in the Mediterranean would keep the fleet in European waters and not dispatch it six thousand miles away to guard against a Japanese attack that might never come, bolstering French morale. The flaw in this logic was that, if a Mediterranean campaign diverted German resources, it would, of course, divert British and French resources, too. The plan for an offensive against Italy had another, deeper flaw. When Backhouse died unexpectedly of brain cancer only seven months into his tenure as first sea lord, his successor, Admiral of the Fleet Sir Dudley Pound, spotted the flaw as soon as he took office. He summed up the problem of scoring a quick victory over Italy in a letter to the new commander in chief, Mediterranean, Admiral Sir Andrew Cunningham:

> I do not know who gave the politicians the idea that it could be done but it seems they expect it and they are now undergoing the rather painful process of being undeceived. Italy can only be "knocked out" either by her armies being defeated, or by Italy being laid waste by air.
>
> We cannot do either of these things at the beginning of the war.[2]

Yet, the primacy of the Mediterranean-based strategy persisted for want of a better option. Sending a fleet to Singapore would have been the best way to prevent the war from spreading to the Far East. Conversely, keeping the fleet in European waters might well tempt the Japanese to attack and, thereby, invite the nightmare three-front war that would place an intolerable strain on the Allies' limited resources. In the end, the issue was moot because the Italians declared their neutrality in September 1939. Nevertheless, we can see from British pre-war plans that the needs of a looming European war were beginning to trump all other considerations. In 1921, Britain had been forced to abandon the Japanese in order to appease the Americans. In 1939, she had to abandon Australia and New Zealand to hold the line against Hitler. Britain's global commitments were no longer sustainable given her small population and ailing economy. Chamberlain was faced with an impossible choice—defend Britain or defend the empire. He could not do both.[3]

That same January, Chamberlain went to Rome to try and talk Mussolini out of his seeming attachment to Hitler but failed to reach an agreement. France had strongly pushed for a rapprochement with Italy, but Chamberlain found out that Mussolini's price for cooperation with the Allies was Tunisia (at that time a French colony), recognition of his claim to Ethiopia, and other colonial concessions in Africa. Britain and France were not ready to pay that high a price, and it was felt that public opinion in both countries would reject any such concessions. The same problem would emerge later in the year when the British and French approached the Soviet Union for an alliance. Hitler was willing to promise Italy anything she wanted in order to win her friendship. It helped that the territories he promised always belonged to somebody else. After Germany's presumed military victory, Hitler could always divvy up the spoils. He would use the same trick on Stalin in August. The democracies could not hand away their own territory, or that of other nations, without both a public outcry and an undermining of their moral position as peace-loving and nonaggressive states wedded to international law. For his part, Mussolini came away from his encounter with Chamberlain and Lord Halifax sure that the democracies were doomed.[4]

With the approach to Italy rebuffed, Chamberlain began to formulate a clear set of boundaries to hold Hitler in check. In modern political parlance, Chamberlain opted for a policy of containment. First, the Cabinet determined that any invasion of Holland by Germany would automatically be a sufficient cause for Britain to declare war. Then, on February 6, His Majesty's Government finally, belatedly, issued a public guarantee of France's borders. Any attack on France would automatically mean war with Great Britain. Staff talks were initiated between the British and French military establishments. Plans for a British expeditionary force, which had been initiated after Munich, were switched into high gear. The French had been insisting since November 1938 that Britain send substantial land forces to their aid if Germany attacked. The French viewed British Army reinforcements as essential if the Germans drove into Belgium, which they had done in 1914 and were very likely to do again. As much as the British hated admitting it, without France, Britain could not prevent German dominance of all Europe, and without a firm commitment to send troops to the Continent, the French might very well be incapable of holding off a German attack. For their part, the French were just as dependent on the British for survival. It may have been an unhappy marriage, but so long as Germany threatened the peace, Britain and France were wedded to each other.

Chamberlain bucked the trend and fought hard in the Cabinet to retain a limited-liability army of only five field divisions, twelve home-defense Territorial Army divisions, and five antiaircraft gun divisions, but the writing was on the wall. Chamberlain tried to persuade his colleagues and the French that the two nations should adopt a division of labor—France should spend money on her army, Britain on her navy and air force—but this formula no longer held much appeal to his own cabinet and chiefs of staff, and it held none at all to the French. It would take an extraordinary move by Hitler to push Chamberlain into a grudging acceptance of a full-scale Continental commitment. Yet, despite disagreements and Chamberlain's misgivings, it was decided that Britain would, in the future, build the army up to six regular and twenty-six Territorial divisions. Four new battleships, a battlecruiser, and an aircraft carrier were to be laid down within the next two years to augment the five battleships and five aircraft carriers already being built. The Chain Home radar system was to be completed to cover the entire eastern coast of Great Britain, and forty-seven modern fighter squadrons were to be in operation by June 1940. But it would be a mistake to think that Chamberlain was shifting away from diplomacy and toward a policy of confrontation. These forces were to fight a war only as a last resort. He was hoping, from February 1939 until war came in September, to put a greater emphasis on deterring Hitler by establishing clear boundaries that he hoped the German dictator would heed and not cross. He also wanted to create additional military forces to give his diplomatic efforts force. If Hitler would not be reasonable, then he would be forced to see reason. What gave this tougher policy extreme urgency was Hitler's surprise decision to invade Czechoslovakia in March.

By sweeping into Czechoslovakia on March 14, Hitler tore up the Munich Agreements and set Britain adrift. Chamberlain was stunned, angered, and humiliated. Despite still possessing a considerable army, the Czechs gave in without firing a shot, which belies the argument of those who maintain that Czechoslovakia would have put up a serious fight the previous September. What prompted Hitler to take such a drastic step is unclear. His ego was certainly bruised when he was forced to accept a diplomatic solution at Munich rather than the military solution he craved. The terrible strain of German arms production, which was eating up probably a quarter of Germany's gross national product, made the capture of Czech gold and currency reserves very tempting. The Germans were practically bankrupt by 1939, their gold and foreign currency reserves exhausted. In fact, they were reduced to barter arrangements with their Eastern European trading partners, exchanging manufactured goods for food and raw materials. The British took advantage of this by buying up excess Romanian oil production using hard currency. Nevertheless, the fall of Czechoslovakia proved a boon to Germany and provided the Germans with more than gold and foreign currency. The large, modern Skoda armaments works were captured intact (the Czechs did not even bother to blow them up as a small act of defiance against their invaders), and Czech tanks were drafted into Hitler's panzer divisions. British aircraft carrier completion dates were set back because much armor plate had been ordered from Skoda to sheath their decks. These deliveries were, of course, cancelled by the Germans when war came. Czech small arms and ammunition could now be swapped for Hungarian, Romanian, and Yugoslavian raw materials. Germany was considerably strengthened, the Allies diminished.

Chamberlain's response was uncharacteristically incautious, bordering on reckless. Two days after German troops entered Prague, Chamberlain gave a speech to the Conservative Association back in his hometown, Birmingham. He departed from his prepared speech and, to shouts of acclimation, proclaimed, "Any attempt to dominate the world by force is one which the democracies must resist."[5] He did this without formally consulting the Cabinet, although Lord Halifax, the foreign secretary, had goaded him on in private. Two weeks later, he wrote a personal letter to the Polish government pledging that "His Majesty's Government and the French Government would at once lend them all their power" if Poland were attacked by Germany.[6] Chamberlain quickly extended the guarantee of military support to Romania, Greece, and Turkey. In April, the British government announced the introduction of a system of limited conscription to increase the size of the army, a move unprecedented in peacetime British history. Fed up with German demands and German unilateral actions, most Britons applauded. Chamberlain himself was annoyed when British intelligence decrypted German diplomatic messages in which Hitler derided the British prime minister. Churchill and Lloyd George gave the government faint praise but demanded that more be done, including the formation of an alliance with Soviet Russia. Chamberlain attempted to obtain from Poland, the Soviet Union, and France an agreement by which they would collectively guarantee the currently existing borders of Europe and consult on "joint resistance" if Germany moved again. The Poles refused, and the Soviets insisted that they would not sign on until the Poles and the French had done so first.[7] Despite this initial setback, Chamberlain persisted in trying to pull together an anti-German alliance, but it would not prove easy.

Chamberlain remained as committed to peace as he had ever been. But his strategy had altered. Chamberlain saw that Hitler had not respected British reason and British fair play, so he was now to be shown British resolve and what Chamberlain believed would soon be an unbeatable, British-led alliance that would check further German aggression. Chamberlain had finally become convinced that Hitler was a ruthless man, but he clung to the hope that he was not necessarily an irrational one. He told the Cabinet that, in a future crisis, "We would attack Germany not to save any particular nation but to pull down a bully."[8] With Rearmament proceeding at a gallop, with the French firm allies— perhaps, in time, the Poles and Russians, too—and with a growing consensus developing at home to stand firm against aggression, it was hoped that Hitler would be dissuaded from attempting any more reckless adventures. He was not.

On hearing of the British pledge to Poland, Hitler was livid. He was offended, not deterred. Plans were put in motion for an invasion of Poland not later than September 1, 1939. Poland herself was as uneasy about war as she was loathe to get involved in what the leaders in London and Paris saw as an inevitable alliance with the Soviet Union. Poland had only wrested her independence from Russia in 1918 and had fought a war against the Soviet Union in 1919–1920. The Poles hated the Russians at least as much as they feared the Germans, possibly more. The Poles were also proud and cocky. Since Poland had beaten the Red Army in the early 1920s, her generals thought that they could, at least for a short time, hold off a German invasion long enough so that Allied pressure from the West would force the Germans to redeploy their army to counter the British and French. We forget now that the German Army in 1939 was completely untested and had not fought a war in over twenty years. The Poles thought that their million-strong army could temporarily handle the Germans, but their Western allies were not so sure. They would have preferred that the Polish government allow Soviet troops to cross into Poland and join the fight against Germany. Although the English and French could accept with equanimity the idea of having Soviet troops pour into Poland to attack the Germans, the Poles adamantly refused to have any Soviet troops entering their country, fearing that once they got in, they would never leave. German planners, however, could not take the Poles' refusal to allow Russian forces to enter their country for granted. To erase the threat of Soviet intervention, Hitler would pull off his greatest diplomatic coup later in the year.

In the short run, with Anglo-German relations in tatters and a war looming with Poland, Hitler cemented his southern flank. Mussolini, desperate for a public relations victory and angry that Hitler had not consulted him when he marched on Prague, invaded Albania in April 1939. Hitler saw this act as ruling out any rapprochement between Mussolini and the Allies while driving Italy further into his camp. He sent his new foreign minister, Joachim von Ribbentrop, a former champagne merchant and enthusiastic Nazi, to meet with his Italian counterpart for discussions on a formal alliance. The treaty of alliance (which Mussolini grandly dubbed the "Pact of Steel") was signed on May 22. Although Mussolini was worried about war and told the Germans that Italy needed four years of peace to get ready (a timetable many German military and political experts would have agreed with for their own country), he sensed that Hitler was in the ascendant and now was the time to jump on his bandwagon. It would take four bloody years to prove Mussolini wrong.[9] He jumped too soon and backed the wrong horse, a choice that the victor of the Spanish Civil War, Fascist dictator Generalissimo Francisco Franco, avoided. Although courted by the Nazis, Franco stayed aloof. Yet, from Hitler's perspective in 1939, Italy was now safely onboard. The Allies would have to worry about defending their position in the Mediterranean during any future crisis. But if Hitler were to satisfy his dream of absorbing Poland into his Reich, he would have to do something about the Soviet Union.

If Hitler and Mussolini's Pact of Steel was not bad enough news for the British, they were soon confronted with trouble in Asia. In June, the Japanese Army clamped a blockade on the British concession at Tientsin, China. Britain had been granted, under the unequal treaties of the nineteenth century, a number of enclaves within major Chinese cities called concessions. These areas were trade zones under British administration where British, not Chinese, law applied. After the Japanese invasion of China, most of Britain's concessions were engulfed by Japanese-occupied territory. The Japanese Army wanted to oust the British from these concessions as they were both an economic nuisance and a window onto Japanese excesses in occupied China. How far the Japanese were prepared to go in their efforts was unclear in London, but the blockade of Tientsin was obviously a test of British resolve. Faced with the overt military alliance of Italy and Germany, British policymakers were wary of pressing the Japanese. The chiefs of staff told the government to seek a diplomatic settlement. Lord Chatfield, the minister for the coordination of defense, told the Cabinet that, if a fleet were to be dispatched to Singapore to signal the Japanese that Britain meant business, the Royal Navy would have to strip the Mediterranean of all British warships and abandon that vital trade route to the mercy of Fascist Italy. The Home Fleet would have to stay put in order to check the Germans, so all of the Mediterranean Fleet would be needed in Asia. Given these prospects and the new emphasis on a Mediterranean strategy to defeat Italy early in the coming war, a diplomatic solution became imperative. Unable to wrest a firm commitment from the Americans that they would go to war against Japan if Britain were forced to, the British ambassador in Tokyo was instructed to work out whatever deal he could. The British were able to come away from the negotiations issuing only a statement that they acknowledged the "special requirements" of the Japanese Army in its dealings with China. This defused the situation. What really aided the British cause was that the Imperial Japanese Navy wanted to avoid war at that time and that the Army got itself tied up in a border skirmish with the Soviets in Mongolia that went dreadfully badly.[10] This induced the Japanese to back away from a war with Great Britain. But the "nightmare scenario" of a simultaneous war against Germany, Italy, and Japan looked ever more likely, and its implications terrified the leaders in London. They could neither fight all three powers simultaneously nor find a price Britain could pay that would buy one or more of them off. Whatever may be said of Neville Chamberlain, it is undeniable that the task he faced was extraordinarily difficult. He needed at least two more years of peace for Rearmament to get him into a position where he might just be able, with French help, to guard both Britain and the empire. But time was running out.

Of all the things Chamberlain was harried into in 1939, none was less palatable to him than the bid for an alliance with the Soviet Union.[11] Chamberlain despised and distrusted the Communists, and they returned the favor. He acknowledged that an alliance with the Soviets was necessary to deter German aggression but hoped it could be confined to the level of a general agreement to come to each other's defense in a war initiated by Nazi Germany. In other words, he wanted a pledge of mutual support, but at no cost to Great Britain or her allies in Eastern Europe. He saw such a deal as beneficial to both the Soviets and himself and could never understand why they did not see it that way, too. Stalin thought the British needed him more than he needed them. Yet, despite Chamberlain's reservations about the Soviet Union, public and parliamentary opinion, along with sound strategic calculation, favored an alliance with Stalin. An Anglo-French delegation made three diplomatic proposals involving military cooperation between the signatories to the Soviet government between June 2 and July 1; all were rebuffed. Ironically, these failures led the old anti-

Appeasement crowd, who had berated Chamberlain for his concessions to Berlin, to clamor ever louder that any and all concessions Moscow demanded must be made in order to get the Soviets to agree to a treaty. Chamberlain and his cabinet were not yet that desperate. They still believed war could be avoided, so the Soviet alliance was important to them but not essential. They knew that what Stalin would want—a free hand in Eastern Europe and a pledge to defend him in any war against Germany, even one he started—was too high a price. Chamberlain felt no compelling need to give the Communists carte blanche. However, that summer Hitler was considering the possibility that he just might be willing to give Stalin what he wanted, if it meant that he could have his war against Poland. A diplomatic revolution was in the offing.

Herman Goering, Hitler's right-hand man, attempted some back-channel negotiations with the British that summer through intermediaries, but the British government, by July 1939, was still sold on the idea of a defensive alliance with the Soviet Union and had come to distrust any German statements. Responding to a surprise Soviet invitation, a military delegation led by a French general and British Admiral Sir Plunkett Drax arrived in Moscow on August 11 with instructions to hammer out a firm mutual-defense pact. Meanwhile, the Germans were feverishly signaling their interest in direct talks with the Soviets. If Hitler could neutralize Russia, he believed that Britain and France would walk away from their guarantees to Poland, and he would get his war of conquest unmolested. On August 14, German foreign minister Ribbentrop had his ambassador in Moscow ask the Soviets if Ribbentrop might come to the Kremlin to negotiate a nonaggression pact. Stalin now had two anxious suitors. He could name his price. Thereafter, the Anglo-French military mission was treated brusquely, and their talks went nowhere. Soviet marshal Voroshilov, who handled the negotiations, demanded that both Poland and Romania agree to the transit of Red Army troops through their territory if war broke out before the Soviet Union would sign any agreement. The Allied military delegation had no power to speak for the Poles or Romanians, of course, and when the French approached the Poles and begged them to concede, the Poles refused. They would not allow Soviet troops into their country. As the situation deteriorated and war looked imminent, the French government went so far as to tell their delegation to lie to the Soviets and tell them that the Poles had agreed, but these instructions were not carried out. By the third week of August, Stalin had become much more interested in what Hitler had to offer. Although the Anglo-French mission would continue to meet with its Soviet counterparts, any chance for an agreement was lost.

When Ribbentrop came to Moscow, he brought with him a generous offer. Eastern Europe was to be split into spheres of influence and Poland partitioned, with roughly half going to the Germans and half to the Soviets. A commercial treaty was to be concluded in which Germany would exchange manufactured goods (including a new heavy cruiser) for Soviet raw materials. Ribbentrop arrived at the Kremlin on August 23, and to everyone's surprise, Stalin was there to meet him; normally, Stalin stayed in the shadows and dealt with the outside world through intermediaries. It took only a few hours, and one phone call back to Hitler, to cement the deal. Latvia, Estonia, and Lithuania fell within the Soviet sphere. Stalin was given a free hand in his dealings with the Finns. He would get nearly half of Poland once she was defeated. Hitler had paid a price the democracies never could. Chamberlain's dream of containment was dead. Relieved of any fear that the Soviets might intervene to help the Poles, Hitler was free to act. War was now inevitable. Poland was doomed.

Some historians have wondered why the British and French were so dilatory in their dealings with the Soviets in 1939. The answer is not hard to formulate. The Conservative leaders of Britain and France had little love for an alliance with Communist Russia and, therefore, were in no hurry to finalize one. They believed that the Soviets were weak and needed the West more than Britain and France needed them. Therefore, it would undermine the Allies bargaining position if they looked too eager to reach a deal with the Soviets. Britain and France also wanted and needed Polish approval for the agreement and found it impossible to obtain such approval under the conditions stipulated by Voroshilov. Lastly, most Western observers saw the Soviets and Nazis as deadly ideological enemies. The idea that Hitler would cut a deal with Stalin seemed so far-fetched that the Allies did not, despite repeated intelligence warnings of German-Soviet talks, comprehend that they were in a race. On balance, it made perfect sense at the time for the British and French to approach the Soviets in a cautious, unhurried manner. Hitler's unpredictability and flexibility caught the Allies off guard. Mesmerized by Hitler's bold stroke, the British and French watched like sleepwalkers as the final countdown to world war proceeded.

In the hope of somehow convincing Hitler that Britain meant business, on August 25 an Anglo-Polish mutual defense treaty was ratified by Parliament. Colonel Beck, the Polish foreign minister, remained calm and confident. Hitler had been demanding that the free port city of Danzig, which had been ceded to international control by the League of Nations after World War I, be returned to Germany. Poland had unhindered access to Danzig and demanded that it remain an open port under league auspices. German control of Danzig would place Polish trade through the Baltic at the whim of the German dictator. Beck played hardball. He rejected all compromise on the Danzig question, sure that his alliance with Britain and France, and the heroism of the Polish Army, would deter Hitler. Lord Halifax urged him to negotiate with Hitler, but the Poles were intransigent. They would not let Soviet troops in, and they would not bargain with Hitler over Danzig. For all his courage, Beck was a fool. Poland was no match for Germany, the British and the French could never mobilize, organize, and launch an offensive in time to save Poland, and the Nazi-Soviet Pact had sealed his country's fate. In the last week of August, the Poles began calling up reservists just in case the Germans attacked; they were to be caught in the early stages of mobilization when German troops crossed the Polish border at 4:45 a.m. on September 1. The British cabinet met that morning and decided to send a warning (but not a clear ultimatum) to Hitler stating that he must withdraw immediately from Polish territory. The French government, temporarily paralyzed, followed suit. Hitler still believed that they were bluffing.[12]

On September 2, Chamberlain addressed the House of Commons on the growing crisis. Here, he completely lost his way. Chamberlain stated that he was hopeful that the Germans would heed his warning and withdraw from Polish territory and that a peace conference could be convened. This was the only point in his tenure as prime minister where Chamberlain's perception of the situation veered into the delusional. There was no chance that Hitler would back down and withdraw his troops, especially as they were penetrating deep into Poland and had gained mastery of the air. Chamberlain had given peace every chance, but now his opponent would not be denied his war. Hitler had made his choice for war, and Britain would have to follow. Although he still had hope, Chamberlain quickly discerned with his practiced political eye that Parliament and his cabinet were in no mood even to consider compromise. The guarantee to Poland would have to be honored. The French looked on expectantly, waiting for the British to say the word. Although Daladier and Bonnet were incapable of independent action, their advisors, even General Gamelin, were surprisingly resolute. As historian Julian Jackson has noted, "What is remarkable about France in 1939 is not the alleged defeatism and pessimism, which many observers claim to have detected in retrospect, but on the contrary the extraordinary confidence of the French political and military elite that it could win a war, and that to survive as a great power it had to do so."[13]

Chamberlain and the Cabinet duly drafted a proper ultimatum and sent it to the British ambassador in Berlin. He was to deliver it at 9:00 a.m. on August 3 with the expectation that Britain would receive a reply by 11:00 a.m. Soon after, the French ambassador delivered his own ultimatum. Hitler and his entourage were stunned. Hitler had been as delusional as Chamberlain in thinking that war with Britain and France could be avoided after so many public pronouncements and the Anglo-Polish military alliance approved by Parliament. Germany did not reply to either ultimatum. Now, all that remained were the formalities.

September 3 was a Sunday. British warships around the world deciphered a message sent out from the Admiralty only minutes after 11 a.m. It read "TOTAL GERMANY," the signal announcing that hostilities had commenced. In the logbook of the Home Fleet's flagship, the battleship *Nelson*, one can still read this fateful entry made at 11:17 a.m.: "War declared on Germany."[14] Chamberlain went on the BBC radio to speak to the nation and the empire. He told of his efforts to preserve the peace and of the refusal of the Germans to answer his challenge demanding their withdrawal from Poland. He summed up by saying, "Consequently, this country is now at war with Germany."[15] France declared war later that afternoon.

NOTES

1. Joseph Maiolo, *The Royal Navy and Nazi Germany* (New York: St. Martin's Press, 1998), 161.

2. Quotation from Maiolo, *The Royal Navy and Nazi Germany*, 175–76.

3. Churchill in 1941–1942 would try to do both with significant American support and still could not manage it, as was shown in Malaya, Singapore, and Burma.

4. Ernest May, ed., *Knowing One's Enemies: Intelligence Assessment before the Two World Wars* (Princeton, NJ: Princeton University Press, 1984), 347.

5. A. J. P. Taylor, *English History: 1914–1945* (Oxford: Oxford University Press, 1965), 441.

6. Taylor, *English History*, 442.

7. Ernest May, *Strange Victory* (New York: Hill and Wang, 2000), 177–78.

8. Quotation from May, *Strange Victory*, 177.

9. Alan Bullock, *Hitler and Stalin: Parallel Lives* (New York: Vintage, 1991), 602–3.

10. May, *Knowing One's Enemies*, 463–64.

11. This section on the Nazi-Soviet pact is drawn from Donald Cameron Watt, *How War Came: The Immediate Origins of the Second World War, 1938–1939* (New York: Pantheon, 1989), 361–84, 447–61.

12. Taylor, *English History*, 450–51.

13. Julian Jackson, *The Fall of France* (Oxford: Oxford, 2003), 214.

14. James Levy, *The Royal Navy's Home Fleet in World War II* (Basingstoke, UK: Palgrave, 2003), 30.

15. Watt, *How War Came*, 601.

Chapter Seven

EPILOGUE: 1940

APPEASEMENT HAD FAILED TO AVERT WAR, but it had not hindered Britain and France in any significant way in their efforts to begin mobilizing their economies for war in earnest before the first shots were fired in September 1939. Time bought by the capitulation at Munich was well spent. The blame for war now fell exclusively on the shoulders of Hitler, and the societies in both Britain and France went to war overwhelmingly united in their determination to challenge and reverse German aggression. Britain's dominions, wavering in their allegiance in September 1938, quickly and wholeheartedly threw in their lots with the mother country one year later. The Allies looked forward to a long, hard struggle, but one they were finally convinced was justified, inevitable, and winnable.

Britain went to war in 1939 to punish Germany for her unprovoked attack on Poland. The Poles held out for less than a month. Everyone knew, just as they had known about Czechoslovakia in 1938, that Britain could not save her Eastern European friend from defeat and occupation. She could only build up her forces along with the French, await the German attack that was bound to come, and hope that the German thrust could be parried, just as it had been in 1914. Then, in 1941 or 1942, the Allies, after mobilizing their economic and imperial resources, could go onto the offensive, drive the Germans back, and force them to the bargaining table. Poland would be restored, Germany would be forced to jettison Hitler and the Nazis, and, with luck, a better peace than Versailles would be worked out. That was the hope. In the meantime, men were processed into the military services, convoys were initiated to protect merchant shipping, and cruisers were deployed to all oceans to hunt down any German surface raiders that might be prowling the high seas. Plans were put in place to distribute gas masks if air raids commenced, guns and searchlights were manned by Territorial Army troops called to the colors, and city children registered for possible evacuation to the countryside or, if things got totally out of hand, perhaps even to Canada.

Winston Churchill, brought into the government as first lord of the Admiralty as a reward for his consistent anti-German stance, chafed at such a long-term strategy of gradual mobilization and demanded action, and at once. He championed three proposals before the Cabinet. Two were idiotic, and one had real merit—about average for Churchillian schemes. Seeing the Soviets now as virtual allies of Hitler, he argued that troops should be sent to help the Finns fight the Russians. Russia, freed from fear of German interference by the Nazi-Soviet Pact, had callously invaded Finland in late 1939. Churchill believed that sending troops to Finland would rally Norway and Sweden to a democratic crusade against Hitler and Stalin (a rather dubious assessment). As a corollary to his plans to send troops to fight the Soviets in Finland, Churchill additionally backed plans devised by the French to bomb the Soviet oil fields in Azerbaijan from

Men too experienced and intelligent to be overly optimistic or ebulliently confident (that is, except for Churchill). The British War Cabinet of September 1939. Standing (from left to right): Lord Hankey, Leslie Hore-Belisha, Winston Churchill, and Sir Kingsley Wood; seated (from left to right): Lord Chatfield, Sir Samuel Hoare, Neville Chamberlain, Sir John Simon, and Lord Halifax (courtesy of Hulton-Deutch Collection/CORBIS).

British-occupied northern Iraq. Given that British and French forces were inadequate at that moment to defeat Germany, bringing the Soviet Union into the war on Nazi Germany's side would have proved suicidal.

The second bad idea Churchill championed was to send ships into Norwegian waters to mine her coastal shipping lanes. Germany got much of her high quality iron ore from Sweden. In the winter, the Baltic Sea was choked by ice, so the iron ore had to be shipped by railroad from northern Sweden to the Norwegian port of Narvik, loaded onto ships, then transported down Norway's Atlantic coast to German ports. Problem was, Norway was a neutral country. Unarmed

German merchant ships could, under international law, travel through Norwegian coastal waters at will. Norway refused British demands to "do something" about German shipping traffic along her coast. And given her neutrality, Norway might fight back if British warships violated her territorial waters. Worse, she might ask for German help in repelling any such incursions, or Germany might use the opportunity afforded by the illegal British mining of Norwegian waters as a pretext for invading that country in "self-defense." Anyway, if Britain took steps that trampled Norway's neutral rights, why could Germany not do the same?

The third idea Churchill argued for was the use of Royal Air Force (RAF) bomber planes to drop mines in the Rhine and Roer rivers to disrupt navigation. This idea was very good and struck directly at a major artery within the German war economy. German industry depended heavily on river transportation to deliver bulk goods like coal, so any disruption of German river traffic would have a negative effect on her war economy.

What we see here is Churchill butting into areas of strategy and policy above the normal ken of a first lord. The Norway operation, however ill advised, was a navy operation; therefore, however foolish or illegal it might be, it was within Churchill's competence to raise the issue. The mining of German rivers was RAF business, and the very notion of going to war with the Soviet Union was the prerogative of the prime minister and the foreign secretary. Chamberlain was usually clever enough to shoot Churchill's worst ideas down on their demerits, but Churchill was relentless. His zeal to win the war was laudable. His judgment was, however, suspect. Churchill's personal qualities of tenacity, fearlessness, and faith in victory and his spellbinding oratory made him a hero. He was a huge personality and a dynamic leader. Subsequent historians have latched onto his persona and been mesmerized by it. Erratic, cocksure, often drunk, he had all of the color Chamberlain conspicuously lacked. At least in part, style has triumphed over substance in the historical assessment of the two men. Churchill's vivacity and charm trumped the weary, stiff visage of Chamberlain, a man whose gaze was fixed on a sad future that he had done everything in his power to forestall. For Churchill, war meant a chance for vindication and greatness. He had been banished from high office because of his hostility to labor unions, his opposition to home rule for India, and his big mouth. He was, before war called him back to office, a sixty-five-year-old political has-been. With war, Churchill found himself ordering around the largest navy on Earth. By contrast, for Chamberlain, determined as he was to lead although he lacked the flair for leadership, war augured death, destruction, and the likely dissolution of the British Empire. Ironically, neither man had held his fate in his own hands. Hitler had called the tune. His stupidity brought on a war that wrecked Chamberlain's reputation and made Churchill's.

Churchill's Norway plan was eventually adopted by the Cabinet. In April 1940, British warships mined the approaches to the port of Narvik. Simultaneously, the Germans, tipped by decoded British signals that gave away the British plan, invaded Norway. Churchill's handling of the Campaign was largely disastrous,[1] but Chamberlain took the heat for the debacle. Chamberlain was normally an excellent debater, but his speech making in Commons defending his war policies fell flat. The House of Commons was losing patience with his stolid approach to the war. Chamberlain promised victory, but only in the long haul and at great cost. The members of Parliament wanted more. They wanted dynamism, flash, someone who could lead the nation. Despite surviving a vote of no confidence, Chamberlain sensed which way the wind was blowing. With a crisis looming on the Continent, Chamberlain was sure that the nation needed a national government with representatives of all three major political parties. The Labour Party leadership quickly let it be known that they would not serve under Chamberlain. Chamberlain was now convinced that he had become a lighting rod for interparty hostility and a distraction to the war effort. He resigned on May 10, 1940. Reluctantly, King George VI called on Churchill to form a government. He would have preferred Lord Halifax, but Halifax had no desire for the job.[2]

Churchill was a fighter and, despite his many flaws, was probably what the country wanted, perhaps even needed, at that hour. He said the same things Chamberlain had: he promised no easy victory, only "blood, toil, sweat, and tears." He just said it so much better and with so much more conviction. Chamberlain stayed on in the Cabinet as lord president of the Council and leader of the House of Commons, where he was still popular among the majority of Conservative members. Churchill did not hate Chamberlain or consider him a bad man. He thought he had been wrong about Appeasement. Very soon, Chamberlain would be stricken with cancer. He refused a peerage, even a knighthood, preferring, he said, to go to his grave as plain old Mr. Chamberlain, as his father had. He died on November 9, 1940. Churchill wrote a beautiful note of condolence to Mrs. Chamberlain on November 10 and said of Chamberlain in the House of Commons on November 12 that "Neville Chamberlain acted with perfect sincerity according to his lights and strove to the utmost of his capacity and authority . . . to save the world from the awful, devastating struggle in which we are now engaged."[3] Those were generous and fair words and a noble epitaph. But between the time Chamberlain left the Cabinet due to ill health in August and the day of his death in November, the world he had known had been turned upside down.

On May 10, 1940, as power in London switched hands from Chamberlain to Churchill, Germany launched her anticipated assault.[4] Holland, Belgium, and France were all attacked simultaneously. The Allies had 136 divisions to Germany's 135. They had more tanks and artillery. Despite ex post facto complaints about the pace of rearmament, the Allies matched or exceeded the Germans in every significant category of weapons and in manpower.[5] But the Luftwaffe quickly dominated the air. German armies were better coordinated, working to a uniform offensive doctrine. German tanks were massed in ten panzer divisions, while most allied tanks served in individual tank battalions assigned throughout the armies. General Gamelin, the Allied commander in chief, commanded only the French and British forces (and the British Army only halfheartedly followed his orders if or when they got through the faulty communications system from French headquarters). The Belgians and Dutch were effectively fighting on their own. Holland's twelve divisions were smashed in three days. The Belgians, who had fought so admirably and delayed the German advance on Paris significantly in 1914, were again called on to buy time for the Allies. Gamelin had decided to break with pre-war doctrine and advance into Belgium to the Dyle River. If Belgium's twenty-two divisions could hold the Germans near the border, British and French troops could get into position on the Dyle and cover Brussels and the industrial heartland of northern France. But the advance exposed the British and French armies to fluid operations they were not trained to handle. The Allies were forced to fight encounter battles with the Germans, who were advancing much more quickly than anticipated.

These loose, whirling actions were the antithesis of the methodical battles the French had trained to fight. Always criticized for being too cautious, the French High Command had been too bold. The Belgians did not hold, and in the following melee, the Allies got the worst of it. Some French and British divisions stopped the Germans cold. An especially creditable case was that of the French Second and Third Light Mechanized Divisions, which fought the German Third and Fourth Panzer Divisions to a standstill. But other units were paralyzed by the speed of events. Some French divisions simply disintegrated under the strain. Worse, a powerful German armored thrust burst into the rear of the Allied forces in Belgium. Weak French reserve divisions holding the line of the Meuse River were pummeled by the Luftwaffe and overrun by German tanks and infantry around the town of Sedan. With almost all of the Allies' best units committed to Belgium, seven of Germany's ten panzer divisions had a clear corridor across northern France to the English Channel. German division and corps commanders, sometimes disobeying direct orders, ran ahead, dragging Hitler and the High Command with them. The pace of operations staggered the British and French. Very quickly, they buckled. The British bolted for the coast. The French fired Gamelin, but it was too late to do anything likely to turn the tide. Several French divisions trapped in Belgium fought valiantly and covered the evacuation of the British Expeditionary Force from Dunkirk. It did not help that the Belgians surrendered during the withdrawal to the coast. Without French support, the British Expeditionary Force would have been annihilated. British historians have often neglected to point this out forcefully.

The Losing Team: French General Georges (left) and British General Lord Gort (right), Commander of the British Expeditionary Force, January 1940 (British Official photograph courtesy of the Imperial War Museum).

The British blamed the French for the overarching disaster, the French blamed the British, and both blamed the Belgians. The crisis split the Allies when they needed to pull together as they had in 1914. By June 4, the British had effectively abandoned their Continental allies, the Belgians had surrendered, and the French generals had fallen to pieces under the strain. Some French units fought on. Many saw that all was lost and fled the battle—the British and Belgians had, they reasoned, so why should they not? The French government on June 14 appealed to its oldest friend, the United States, to intervene in any way America could to help aid in France's defense, but the French were soundly rebuffed. France was doomed. Despondent, Prime Minister Paul Reynaud quit. France's new prime minister, the aged Marshal

153

Henri-Philippe Pétain, asked the Germans for an armistice. It was signed on June 22.

For France, one last indignity awaited. After the signing of the armistice, Churchill stabbed her in the back by attacking the exposed French naval squadron at Mers el-Kebir in Algeria. Churchill had insisted that French naval forces disregard the terms of the armistice and either come over to the British or allow themselves to be interred under British control. The French assured him that their fleet would not be handed over to Germany and Italy, but the British ignored their statements. To impress Hitler and Roosevelt with his ruthless determination to fight on and to demonstrate to a nervous and divided Cabinet who was now boss, on July 3 Churchill ordered the attack against the French squadron: 1,297 French officers and sailors were killed, and hundreds more wounded. Admiral Sir James Somerville, who despised the order to attack but felt obliged to obey it, performed his mission halfheartedly, and several French warships escaped the carnage. When the French government bitterly complained to President Roosevelt of this British treachery, Roosevelt callously told them that he would have done the same thing if he were Churchill.[6]

The German victory in May-June 1940 was one of the greatest in military history. It had not been as cheap or easy as it had looked: 43,000 German troops were killed or missing, presumed dead, and 114,000 were wounded in less than six weeks of fighting.[7] At several points, German caution had come close to giving the Allies the time they needed to pull themselves together and form an effective line of defense. The Germans had been rescued by subordinate commanders who took the initiative, often against orders, and kept the momentum of the attack rolling. Speed, daring, and a superior German tactical doctrine had won the day. All of this was the bequest of the little hundred-thousand-man army of the 1920s that had originated Germany's offensive doctrine and filled its officers with the precepts of infiltration and encirclement. The Allied armies, as had always been feared, were not up to the demands of offensive operations or a rapidly changing battlefield environment.

What followed, of course, was the Battle of Britain. The radar and fighter planes Chamberlain had insisted that the RAF procure beat back the Luftwaffe and saved the day. Churchill's bravura leadership also played a key role. Hitler quickly lost interest in the careful, long-term planning and industrial mobilization needed to execute a successful amphibious invasion of Britain. He turned his attention east, to the lands he had coveted for so long in the Soviet Union. Next spring, he thought, they would all be his.

By November 1940, Churchill was requesting unconditional aid from the United States. Churchill had authorized vast purchases of weapons and equipment from the United States upon taking over as prime minister. Six months later, Britain was on the edge of bankruptcy. The fourth arm of defense had withered to a paralytic state. Chamberlain's nightmare of national decline was coming true. American aid came with strings attached that made the United Kingdom a virtual economic satellite of the United States. Effective political and psychological subordination soon followed. Great Britain's time as an independent Great Power had come to an end.

NOTES

1. Correlli Barnett, in his laudable history of the Royal Navy in World War II, *Engage the Enemy More Closely* (New York: Norton, 1991), described Norway as "a Churchillian disaster."

2. See James Levy, *The Royal Navy's Home Fleet in World War II* (Basingstoke, UK: Palgrave, 2003), 62–63 and notes.

3. Martin Gilbert, ed., *The Churchill War Papers*, vol. 2 (New York: Norton, 1995), 1076, 1080–82.

4. The best available accounts are those of Julian Jackson and Ernst May found in the bibliographical essay at the end of this volume.

5. For the most up-to-date statistical breakdown, see Ernest May, *Strange Victory* (New York: Hill and Wang, 2000), 466–80.

6. For a recent appraisal, see Philippe Lasterle, "Could Admiral Gensoul Have Averted the Tragedy of Mers el-Kebir?" *The Journal of Military History* 67 (3): 835–44.

7. John Ellis, *World War II Databook* (London: Aurum Press, 1993), 255.

Chapter Eight

CONCLUSION

APPEASEMENT AND REARMAMENT HAD FAILED to prevent the outbreak of World War II. The joint policies of negotiating for peace while building up the armed forces to deter another war did not work. War was not avoided, and Germany won the opening round of the fighting. In retrospect, would it have been better if another set of policies had been adopted? No. The opponents of Appeasement often stress how Chamberlain failed to understand Hitler's grandiose ambitions and aggressive temperament. They argue that Hitler could not have been appeased, so attempting to do so was folly. Of course, one can never know a thing to be true unless one attempts to find out. Chamberlain wanted to believe that, after all was said and done, Hitler was a German nationalist out for the best deal he could get for his people. Chamberlain set out to test this hypothesis but failed to reckon on how insanely Hitler would eventually act. However, he could not have known for certain about Hitler's insatiable desire for war unless he first tried to deal with him in a reasonable manner. It would have been more than a shame if millions had died if war could have been avoided.

Eventually, Hitler was shown to be not only unreasonable but also irrational; he invaded Poland, and Britain and France declared war.

Yet, if the enemies of Appeasement are correct in assuming that war was inevitable, then Appeasement did not matter. Appeasement did not stop the war, but it did not cause the war either. In 1934, Hitler was checked in his efforts to force a unification of Germany with Austria. This did not stop him from coming back in 1938 and annexing Austria. At Munich, Hitler did not get all of Czechoslovakia, as he secretly desired. In March 1939, he marched in just the same and grabbed it. If Hitler could not be appeased, it is extremely unlikely that he could have been deterred. Throughout his career, he never was. War was inevitable because Hitler wanted it that way. He could never have been "stopped," not at the Rhineland, not at Munich, not anywhere. Sooner or later, he would push too far and war would come. It did come when he overstepped himself and invaded Poland despite clear warnings that war would follow. Would a clearer warning in 1938 have deterred him? One doubts it. As historian Robert Young has pondered, "How to deal with someone [Hitler] who, wittingly, has painted himself into a corner? Compromise is as futile as intimidation in the glazed eyes of the deranged."[1] Would a war have gone better in 1938 than it did in 1939? Perhaps, but we have seen that such a claim is doubtful and takes little account of the real military situation. Counting divisions is not enough. You have to look at levels of training, the military doctrines of the different powers, their command styles, weaponry, and the internal cohesion of the states. With Poland and Hungary effectively backing Germany, with the Red Army decapitated by the purges and having no land bridge to Czechoslovakia, and with the British and French neither willing nor able to take the offensive, September 1938 may well have unfolded the same way September 1939 did. So, again, was there an alternative to Appeasement and Rearmament as dual strategies for dealing with the strategic situation of the 1930s? I will summarize here my argument that, for both practical and moral reasons, the answer is no.

On a practical level, Appeasement and Rearmament were logical and appropriate strategies for the 1930s. They took account of the general sentiment of a British electorate that wanted neither war nor a militarized society. They conformed to the economic orthodoxy of the time that demanded balanced budgets and limited government interference in the private sector of the economy. Appeasement and Rearmament together reflected the needs of a global empire whose financial and industrial resources were no longer adequate to face a global challenge. Britain needed to cozy up to her few friends and limit the number of her potential enemies. Britain's most powerful likely enemy was Germany. Chamberlain wanted to reach an accommodation with her for the overwhelmingly practical reason that war was not in Britain's interest and would in all probability leave the British Empire so weakened that the demands of Italy, Japan, and even Russia would be impossible to resist. Britain needed time to recover economically and militarily from the debt burden left from fighting World War I, the defense cuts of the 1920s and early 1930s, and the ravages of the Great Depression. Appeasement was the only policy that could buy that time. If a reasonable settlement was reached with Germany, so much the better. It was Hitler who refused a reasonable settlement. It was Hitler who started the war. What Chamberlain got wrong was his estimation of Hitler's willingness to take an unwarranted risk when he could have secured an excellent deal. It was just astonishing to Chamberlain that anyone could throw away the kind of deal he envisioned for Germany—the unification of all ethnic Germans under one German government, negotiated armaments treaties, perhaps even colonial concessions—so that they could roll the dice in an all-or-nothing bid to rule Europe. Frankly, Chamberlain simply refused to believe it, and he refused to believe it past the point where it was obvious. But Chamberlain was right in thinking that the Germans could not, in the long run, pull off their bid for Eurasian supremacy. What he most feared was that the Germans would take Britain down with them in their suicidal bid for hegemony. That is why he so desperately hung on to the policy of Appeasement: not out of a misguided affection for Germany, or some secret admiration for fascism, but in a desperate attempt to defend his own beloved country's independent Great Power status.

Appeasement eventually showed just who the aggressors really were. In going to war only after all else had failed, the Allies gained a moral credibility that they would not have enjoyed if they had waged a preventative war. This gave the Allied cause an untarnished glow it has never lost. German aggression after Munich helped sway public opinion inside and outside Europe against Germany, which helped win the war. The support of the Dominions and the United States would have been much harder to procure in 1938 than it was in 1939 after Hitler's seizure of Prague and unprovoked attack on Poland.

By 1939, Rearmament in Britain was in full swing. It was proceeding about as fast as was possible in a democratic state in peacetime, absorbing about 12.5 percent of Britain's gross national product. Taxes were raised, bonds issued, and men conscripted into the service. This was not what Chamberlain had wanted, but he did it nonetheless. He had hoped for a more gradual pace of rearmament that would deter Hitler and prevent war if Appeasement failed. We must remember that Appeasement was a dual policy that aimed primarily to prevent war and only secondarily to delay it. Rearmament was likewise a dual policy to deter war first and to create the means to fight a war only secondarily. It was hoped that the general settlement of grievances in Europe would be influenced by Rearmament; the stronger Britain grew militarily, the more effective her diplomacy would be. In all of this, we can lose sight of the fact that everyone in Britain, even Churchill, wanted to avoid war. The question was how best to do this. So, the broadest question facing the British was how they thought about war: was it just another instrument of foreign policy or an evil to be avoided? Then, people had to ask themselves, Given our answer to this question, what is the best way to prevent war if we think that it is an evil to be avoided? Conversely, if war is just another tool for achieving a favorable end, when is the best time to start one in order to achieve our policy goal? These crucial questions got confused in the 1930s and have remained confused ever since. Here we shall try to untangle them.

The hawks, like Churchill, thought that war was an instrumentality in the arsenal of states and that the best way to prevent war was to be able to fight one successfully at any time. They wanted massive military spending and an aggressive foreign policy. The problem here was that France was not willing to play this game, and the British Army, for political, financial, and cultural reasons, could never be built up to a size and power where it could simply land in northern Germany and dictate terms to Hitler. The backstop of any aggressive British foreign policy had to be the French Army, and the French Army expected to be outnumbered and did not consider itself a match for the Germans in a war of maneuver. The French Army wanted to fight a defensive war, and that implied a defensive foreign policy. An aggressive British foreign policy was doomed without active, enthusiastic French assistance, a level of support the French would not give without ironclad British guarantees of military and financial support. These guarantees the British government and public were unable or unwilling to give. Therefore, an aggressive British foreign policy lacked credibility because Britain alone could not carry it out. If Hitler called England's bluff, she would be stuck fighting the war British policy was supposed to prevent without much chance, at least in the short term, of winning it.

Conversely, the Labour Party advocated collective security through the League of Nations as a means to keep the peace. This policy had merit. It was not overtly aggressive but could be made tough enough if the nations of the league pulled together to thwart aggression. Working together, especially with the Soviet Union, an anti-Hitler alliance could preserve the peace and keep Hitler under wraps. The problems here were twofold. Trying to coordinate nations like Russia, France, and Poland was like trying to herd cats. They would not go where you wanted them. And the Labour Party consistently voted against increased arms expenditures and conscription. They refused to grasp that other nations had no interest in allying themselves to Britain in an anti-Hitler coalition if they were going to do all of the fighting and dying while the British cheered their high moral efforts from the sidelines. If Britain could not pull its weight militarily, nobody was going to jump on her anti-Hitler bandwagon.

What was to be done? Britain had to try to avoid war but be strong enough to bargain effectively and attract allies so that she could fight if she had to. Most men in high policy circles in government and the British military were convinced that war would likely bankrupt the country and leave the empire prey to other powers. However, complete surrender of continental Europe to the Germans would be unacceptable and dangerous. Some accommodation would have to be reached with Germany, Italy, or Japan. If such a deal could not be hammered out, then Britain would need a much bigger military establishment and reliable allies. The optimal solution to the problem was to use diplomacy and increased military spending in tandem. Appeasement would perhaps solve the problem and would certainly buy time for Rearmament. Rearmament would lend weight to diplomacy and be essential in the worst-case scenario of an all-out war. The very structure of the problem dictated the policies—Appeasement and Rearmament—that were in fact adopted. On practical grounds, Chamberlain's approach was the correct one.

Now we must address the moral issues raised by Appeasement. The most powerful element of the moral case against Appeasement involves the Holocaust. Using the Holocaust as a case against Appeasement is a common practice. It is also a pure example of ex post facto justification, which anyone who has studied logic knows to be a very weak premise to begin with. Let's look at the case anyway. The argument is that if Hitler had been "stopped" in 1936 or 1938, then the Holocaust would never have happened, and 5.7 million Jews murdered by the Nazis would never have been killed. This argument is predicated on three assumptions: that everyone knew the Holocaust was coming and therefore can be held morally responsible for not acting to prevent it; that the Allies could have beaten Germany quickly in 1936 or 1938; that the Nazis would not have taken the opportunity offered by the Allies' defensive strategy to conquer Czechoslovakia and perhaps Romania to grab their raw materials. Such a move into Czechoslovakia and Romania would have placed the lives of hundreds of thousands of their Jewish citizens in grave danger. The premise that the Holocaust was obviously in the offing is hotly debated by historians and not well supported by the evidence of the time. Nazi persecution of Jews was not equated with a plan for their extermination. The Nazis first choice in the 1930s had always been expulsion. The second assumption, that the Allies would have won decisively in 1936 or 1938, is belied by their performance in 1940 and, I have shown, is quite unlikely. That the Allies' defensive strategy would have allowed the Nazis to get their hands on more Jews than the two hundred fifty thousand who still lived in Germany in 1939 (half had emigrated in the six preceding years) is very likely indeed. The vast majority of Europe's Jews lived in Eastern Europe and the Soviet Union. So long as war was avoided, Eastern Europe's Jews were as safe as people can be under largely dictatorial regimes. Once war commenced, if it could not be won quickly, then those people would be placed at vastly greater risk. In fact, the historical record shows that Jews were not systematically murdered by the Nazis until after a general war broke out in 1939; they were persecuted in Austria and, later, in the Czech lands, but the mass murder could only be justified and covered up by war. So, if war came, the Jews of Europe could only be saved if Germany was defeated. Realistically, Britain and France could not defeat Germany before 1941 at the earliest. Victory was nearly impossible without Rearmament, and Rearmament needed time. Therefore, given the circumstances, Appeasement was necessary to buy that time. What was unnecessary was the policy of Britain, France, the United States, Canada, and many other countries that refused entry to Jews who would have gladly left Germany, Austria, and other countries occupied or threatened by Hitler. Here was a true moral failure because the cost of helping was not a world war, just some resettlement money and a few angry anti-Semitic voters. This moral failure cannot be easily explained and was, in reality, inexcusable.

On a more abstract level, how do we condone making compromises with evil? When does one cut cards with the devil? And would you know him if you met him? Certainly, in 1938 Joseph Stalin had as much claim to the title "Prince of Darkness" as Hitler did. Yet, most opponents of Appeasement who castigated Chamberlain then and condemn him now for surrendering to evil argue for signing on with one devil (Stalin) in order to beat the other. Too many historians have been fishing in murky waters and imagining they see clearly to the bottom. They condemn Chamberlain for conciliating Hitler, then turn around and condemn him for not allying himself with Stalin, a mass murderer of unimaginable proportions. Is it because, since we later saw the pictures from the camps, we have faces to place on the corpses of Hitler's vast toll of victims, while most of those who died in Stalin's Russia are, to us, nameless, faceless peasants? Who knows? But to say that in 1938 or 1939 the choice between the two evils was clear is monstrously wrong.

We somehow have to rise above the confusion and vitriol and seek some moral position from which to argue these issues. In the end, it comes down to the two clear approaches to war that we have already identified. Either war is an evil to be avoided at all costs, or at great costs, or it is merely an amoral tool.[2] I say two choices rather than three because the first two—avoid war altogether or avoid war as long and as strongly as you can—both take war to be a moral or social evil, whereas the third view—war is just another means of settling disputes—places no value judgment on war per se.

A pacifist would argue that war is under almost any circumstances an evil to be avoided. Others, and Chamberlain was of this school, see war as an evil that must be avoided at great cost but not at all costs; it must be the last resort of the reasonable man. Many people disagree. War in many peoples' minds is an instrumentality to be judged on utilitarian grounds. It exists in the realm of cost-to-benefit analysis. War is invoked when the benefits clearly outweigh the costs. An example: In 1956, the people of Hungary revolted against their Communist government. The Central Intelligence Agency had encouraged this action. Soviet troops responded, the Hungarian rebels were put down, and perhaps a hundred thousand people died. The United States did nothing. So, why do people not run around invoking "Budapest" the way they do "Munich" and condemn President Dwight D. Eisenhower as a coward and a fool for "not standing up against evil" the way they often vilify Neville Chamberlain? Perhaps because everyone knew that the whole cold war exercise in Hungary was being played out on a cynical stage of power politics between two regimes (in Washington, D.C., and Moscow) where utilitarian calculations mattered most. But out of Munich, because Hitler turned out to be so evil, people have constructed a morality play. The expectation was that Chamberlain should have played a different role in 1938 than Eisenhower did in 1956. The rationale for condemning Chamberlain is, therefore, that Chamberlain should have sacrificed his nation's money and lives to the battle of good against evil. Everyone in 1956 knew that a nuclear World War III would kill millions. Americans knew that millions of those dead would be themselves and their families. It's a lot easier to castigate the British for not risking millions to save the Czechs than it is to risk your own family to save the Hungarians. You just change the terms of the debate. You make Munich a moral issue and Budapest a practical one. Thereby, Chamberlain can be cast in the role of the immoral appeaser, while Eisenhower was merely a prudent statesman.

Such slight of hand is very useful. If practical considerations do not sway public opinion, give the people a moral crusade. Can't sell Vietnam on the "Domino Principle"? Tell the folks you are standing up for freedom. However, it is clear from history that the U.S. government flip-flops between moral considerations and practical ones because it is easy for policymakers to confuse the issues in their own minds and because the mix has a broader appeal than either justification alone. A useful example of how such issues get played out (and confused) in the real world is the Iraq War of 2003. In 1956, the United States did not act because the cost of helping the Hungarians was out of all proportions to the benefit of liberating them. In 2003, the United States was content to go to war against Iraq because Iraq was pitiably weak and the benefits of war (military bases, pressure on the Palestinians, oil, distraction from a poor economy, misplaced but sweet, and politically popular, revenge for the World Trade Center attack) outweighed the costs (international antipathy, some thousands of U.S. and many more thousands of Iraqi lives, at least $100 billion). If the practical justification seems to evaporate (the imminent threat of Iraqi chemical and biological weapons), switch to the moral crusade of "liberating the Iraqi people." Or throw them both out, along with several other possibilities, and keep switching the justification until something sticks. This is the utilitarian view of international relations writ large. Yet, it would probably be unjust to think that President George W. Bush clearly perceives the difference between cold strategic motivations and his own deeply held personal convictions about the justness of his cause and that he understands his actions as blatant manipulation. People often believe what they want to believe and fit evidence to match their preconceptions. But in the end, for the U.S. government as an institution, it does not matter how you get what you want, at home or abroad, so long as the goal is accomplished.

But we have only tangentially gotten at the moral issue. Is war acceptable if it is cheap but unthinkable if it is costly? Or can another set of values be brought to bear? Chamberlain, we must remember, was not offered a cheap war. Hitler was most certainly not Saddam Hussein. But the issue starts to clarify itself: war as utility versus war as moral dilemma. If it is a utilitarian issue, Chamberlain may or may not have miscalculated in 1938. The preponderance of evidence says to me that he did not. But if it is a moral question, then we are faced with a "lesser of two evils" choice (if we accept war as a necessary evil). Is it more moral to stand up to evil or to preserve the peace? When does one concern outweigh the other? Here individuals can only take their best guess. Is war a terrible necessity given the jungle of international relations, or is it a powerful tool to be used for the betterment of the state? The international arena of sovereign states is a Wild West town without a lawman. We may all be called on to shoot our neighbors if things get out of hand. The moral question of invoking war has to do with when it is okay to shoot your neighbor. Is it fine to kill him when you see him gathering arms into his house, when he crosses into your yard armed to the teeth, or simply if he has a nicer car than you do and you want it? Wars are fought for all three reasons: preventative wars, wars of self-defense, and wars for conquest. Philosophers and theologians have wrestled with these issues for centuries. When is a war "just"? By traditional definition, World War II was a just war because one side (the Allies) was defending itself against unprovoked aggression after all steps to mediate the dispute, short of war, had been tried and had failed and because not fighting would be worse for humanity than allowing the aggressors to take what they wanted without opposition. On all counts, Chamberlain's policy comes out in full accord with the traditional Christian criteria for a just war. What historian and essayist Gwynne Dyer has written of another conflict is just as true for World War II: "It just seems really stupid and vicious to make it [war] happen one minute before you're certain that it absolutely has to happen."[3] Or, as Chamberlain said, "War is a fearful thing, and we must be very clear, before we embark on it, that it is really the great issues that are at stake."[4]

Yet, the issues of war and peace have a deeper philosophical implication that makes an absolute judgment on the moral implications of Appeasement nearly impossible to adjudicate. Unless some deity addresses the United Nations General Assembly or hyperintelligent aliens land on the White House lawn and dispense the answer, we cannot know the absolute definition of a just war for sure. I can define what I mean by a just war, then use that set of criteria to judge government action. But what if others use a different set of criteria? What if the national leadership defines a just war as one that may *potentially* save American lives in the long run? I can argue that such a definition is not the one that has been traditionally used for defining a just war, but so what? I stick to my definition, and they stick to theirs. It comes down to a matter of individual moral choice. We have no universally accepted set of moral absolutes.[5] Even if we believe in the Judeo-Christian invocation "Thou shalt not kill," we can get no consensus between and among Jews and Christians as to what that commandment means, when it applies, or to whom it applies. In reviewing the decisions of Baldwin, Daladier, and Chamberlain in the 1930s, we can only try to discern how they thought about these issues. We can reject their choices, but without a universal frame of moral reference, we cannot refute them on moral grounds. It is impossible to "prove" that Chamberlain was morally correct in believing that war was so terrible it must be avoided until no other choice presented itself. This author can simply try to persuade the reader that, in his opinion, Chamberlain took a right moral course. Better still, this work invites the reader to reflect upon those times and draw his or her own conclusions. All one can do, once he or she has come to some principled position, is to be consistent. This is very hard, as we have seen. People purposely confuse the issues to gain points in debate or push their own agendas. All that the historian can say is that, for some very sound strategic and moral reasons, Chamberlain and his cabinet chose to avoid war right down to the point where Hitler forced their hands. It is highly likely that Chamberlain did this, at least in part, due to an internal moral choice against war. This book has argued that he chose correctly. Others disagree. It is in wrestling with such difficult choices that our assumptions about the world, and ourselves, are exposed. It is in the act of choosing that we discover what we believe.

In the moral dilemma between preventing the evil of war and confronting the evil of Hitler, Chamberlain in 1938 chose to avoid war. In 1939, he was forced to switch to confrontation. He did not want to. He had done everything he could in good faith to prevent war, and, yet, war came. Chamberlain just could not stop Hitler from being Hitler. The Nazis had made the first move, and now everyone knew their true colors and became convinced that German aggression had to be opposed. All reasonable attempts to dissuade

Hitler from his course had failed. It would be hard to argue that a reasonable alternative remained because Hitler had left Britain and France without any credible alternative in September 1939. Heartbroken, Chamberlain took his country to war. He was right to do so.

NOTES

1. Robert J. Young, *France and the Origins of the Second World War* (New York: St. Martin's Press, 1996), 102.

2. A fourth possibility is to consider war a positive social good. Hitler believed this, but such a position has fallen out of favor or, at least, is no longer discussed in polite society.

3. Quotation from Gwynne Dyer's essay "The Time-Table," January 31, 2003, available at www.gwynnedyer.net.

4. Quotation from Ernest May, *Strange Victory* (New York: Hill and Wang, 2000), 178.

5. For a discussion of how and why a universal moral code seems impossible to formulate, see Richard Rorty, *Contingency, Irony, and Solidarity* (Cambridge: Cambridge University Press, 1989).

BIBLIOGRAPHIC ESSAY

THE LITERATURE ON BRITAIN AND FRANCE in the 1930s is immense. Some material is strikingly good, but most has an ax to grind. Much ink was spilled during and after World War II assigning blame for the disastrous defeat of Britain, France, and the Low Countries in 1940. This blame game makes it imperative that readers suspend judgment and consult multiple sources before drawing firm conclusions about the period. Ideology has also played a big part in shaping the historiography of the period. However, the way historians have been affected by ideology as they have drawn our current picture of Appeasement does not break into the usual Left-Right dichotomy. Nevertheless, political battles in the late 1940s, 1950s, and 1960s over how to deal with the Soviet Union colored much that was written about Chamberlain and Appeasement. Whether you believed in containing communism or "rolling it back," you were opposed to Appeasement and castigated Chamberlain for "giving in" to an aggressor. If you were a die-hard anti-Communist and wanted that system destroyed, you bought the line that Hitler had only succeeded because Chamberlain had been "weak" and conciliatory. But, if you were on the other side of the political spectrum and were for détente with the Soviets, or even supported them, you denigrated those appeasers who had made deals with evil fascism. So, Left and Right could agree, for their own policy reasons, if not because of the historical record, that "Munich" and Appeasement were things to be anathematized. The Holocaust also provided a reference point for Nazi evil that made those who had tried to deal reasonably with Hitler in the 1930s appear suspect at best, as collaborators in mass murder at worst. Only recently have historians been in a position to sidestep these highly charged issues and not read history backward from the Berlin blockade and Auschwitz to Munich and the Rhineland. The following works either pioneered the effort to place the 1930s in their unique historical context or have largely taken for granted that men are not clairvoyant. This author has relied heavily on their research and is greatly in their debt, even if many of these historians would not necessarily agree with all or parts of his thesis.

Of inestimable value in considering Appeasement and Rearmament in their broadest political, strategic, and economic contexts are the works of Paul Kennedy. His *Rise and Fall of British Naval Mastery* (Ashfield Press, 1986) and *Rise and Fall of the Great Powers* (Vintage, 1989) show how Britain's weakening economic grip and relative decline, compared to Germany, the United States, and Soviet Russia, contributed to the instability of the early twentieth century. Although he would certainly not agree with all of the conclusions reached about the period in this book, his work has influenced this author greatly. Eric Hobsbawm's *Industry and Empire* (Weidenfield and Nicholson, 1968) pioneered a basically economic approach to understanding British policy in the inter-war years. Hobsbawm argues persuasively that the British Empire by 1938 had no clothes. His thesis helped wrest the narrative of the late 1930s from the hands of the diplomatic historians, who were often wrapped up in the minutiae of negotiations and at times poorly informed about the broader military and economic context of decision making. Hobsbawm's later work *The Age of Extremes* (Pantheon, 1994) also has much to say about the crisis years leading up to World War II. A complementary voice, though one made uneasy by what he calls the "economic determinism" of Kennedy, can be found in B. J. C. McKercher's *Transition of Power: Britain's Loss of Global Pre-eminence to the United States, 1930–1945* (Cambridge University Press, 1999). For a fascinating framework for any discussion of war, I would recommend Gwynne Dyer's *War* (Crown, 1985).

Of general interest is Clive Ponting's *Armageddon* (Random House, 1995) if for no other reason than his determination to take no part of the received "truths" about World War II for granted. Also of great value in understanding those times is Alan Bullock's *Hitler and Stalin: Parallel Lives* (Vintage, 1991). I have learned much about Germany and the Soviet Union from his analysis of these men and their policies. For France, one can read *France and the Origins of the Second World War* (St. Martin's Press, 1996) by a true expert in this field, Robert J. Young. His earlier book, *In Command of France: French Foreign Policy and Military Planning* (Harvard University Press, 1978), was instrumental in provoking a general reappraisal of the period. And for a splendid overview of Britain in the 1930s, A. J. P. Taylor's *English History: 1914–1945* (Oxford University Press, 1965) is recommended. Taylor's book is funny, smart, opinionated, and readable. The immediate run-up to war is covered in exquisite detail by Donald Cameron Watt in his *How War Came: The Immediate Origins of the Second World War, 1938–1939* (Pantheon, 1989). However, the older, controversial *Origins of the Second World War* (Athenaeum, 1966) by A. J. P. Taylor should also be consulted for its insights and provocations.

The military aspects underlying strategy and diplomacy in the 1930s have been blessed with much original scholarship in recent years. For Britain, all considerations of the period must begin with N. H. Gibbs's *Grand Strategy*, Volume I (Her Majesty's Stationary Office, 1976). Gibbs combines the penetrating mind of an Oxford don with rigorous archival research in mapping out the course of British Rearmament. Secondarily, he tackles the issue of the interplay between military preparedness, strategy, and diplomacy. His book is brilliant if a bit slow going. Of equal weight is G. C. Peden's *British Rearmament and the Treasury* (Scottish Academic Press, 1976), which shows how financial constraints, tax policy, and balance-of-payments concerns interacted with the British rearmament effort. For another good overview of Britain's strategic commitments, with a special emphasis on imperial policing in the 1920s and 1930s, see Anthony Clayton, *The British Empire as a Superpower 1919–39* (University of Georgia Press, 1986).

Turning to the more strictly military side of Rearmament, one should start with Stephen Roskill's two-volume *Naval Policy between the Wars* (Collins, 1968, 1976), still the standard overview. However, in recent years, three books have immensely broadened and deepened our understanding of the inter-war Royal Navy: Andrew Gordon's *British Seapower and Procurement between the Wars* (Naval Institute Press, 1988), Joseph Maiolo's *The Royal Navy and Nazi Germany* (St. Martin's Press, 1998), and Christopher M. Bell's *The Royal Navy, Sea Power and Strategy between the Wars* (Stanford University Press, 2000). All three are detailed scholarly histories that mine Admiralty records for an understanding of how the Royal Navy saw its job, what steps it took to meet the challenge of the 1930s, and why the Royal Navy supported Appeasement. Of equal value in dissecting the attitudes and limitations of the French Army is Eugenia Kiesling's superb *Arming against Hitler* (University of Kansas Press, 1996). Kiesling brilliantly demolishes the myths of a reactionary and befuddled French military establishment shrouded in thoughts of impending doom, listlessly awaiting certain defeat. Of interest here also is Julian Jackson's *The Fall of France* (Oxford, 2003), as well as Ernest R. May's *Strange Victory* (Hill and Wang, 2000).

For short takes on certain aspects of the military forces of all of the major powers in the 1930s, one can consult *The Challenge of Change* (University of Nebraska Press, 2000), edited by Harold R. Winton and David R. Mets. The reader would be advised to begin any enquiry into inter-war intelligence gathering and assessment with Ernest May, editor, *Knowing One's Enemies: Intelligence Assessment before the Two World Wars* (Princeton University Press, 1984). The standard work on the British Army is David French's *Raising Churchill's Army* (Oxford, 2001); French gets to the heart of the problem of the mismatch between Britain's up-to-date combined-arms doctrine and her antique, authoritarian command culture. He also takes a careful look at the way British society shaped her army.

It would be of great value to have a full, modern biography of Neville Chamberlain, but no such book exists. David Dilks has given half of one in his *Neville Chamberlain, Volume I, 1869–1929* (Cambridge University Press, 1984). The best current overview is Graham Stewart's *Burying Caesar: The Churchill-Chamberlain Rivalry* (Overlook Press, 2001). Even this gives pride of place to Winston Churchill, who has been the subject of a staggering number of works, many uncritical, some hagiographic. The more skeptical are referred to the works of Richard Charmley and Correlli Barnett.

Charmley's *Churchill: The End of Glory* (Harcourt, 1993) and Barnett's *The Audit of War* (Macmillan, 1986) have shaken up the field considerably. Also of interest is James Levy, *The Royal Navy's Home Fleet in World War II* (Palgrave, 2003).

The most forceful denunciation of Chamberlain's policy of Appeasement, which this author has attempted to defend, is probably Williamson Murray's *The Collapse of the European Balance of Power* (Princeton University Press, 1984), although the many works of Martin Gilbert and Gerhard Weinberg can also be consulted for their anti-Appeasement views.

INDEX

aircraft carriers, 76, 80
air force: British (RAF), 57, 60, 62,
    66, 68–74, 69, 79, 82, 93–94, 98,
    107, 115, 148, 155; Churchill on
    German, 70–71; Hitler on
    German, 70
Algeria, 154
Allies, World War I, 1–18; reparations
    ordered by, 2–5; victory of, 1–2,
    43, 51
Allies, World War II: Hitler v., 112,
    114, 116, 128, 131–33, 134,
    145–55, 160, 161–65; Japan and,
    127; moral credibility of, 160, 169
Amery, Leo, 91, 121
appeasement: definition of, x, xvin1;
    historical use of, x–xi; Japan and, x;
    U.S. and, x–xi, 115
Appeasement policy, British, ix–x,
    xi–xii, xiv, xv–xvi; arguments
    against, ix–x, xi–xii, 52–53, 85n1,
    125, 157–58, 166; blame placed
    on Chamberlain, Neville, for, xii,
    xiii–xiv, 136–37, 157–58,
    159–61, 163, 165, 166–69, 170;
    Churchill v., xiii, 125; as dual
    policy, 159, 161–63; failure of, x,

xii, xiii–xiv, 130, 134, 139,
    140–42, 145, 157, 159–60, 161;
    guiding principle of, 12; before
    Holocaust, x, xii, xv, 163–65; lack
    of alternatives to, 157–59; military
    support for, 84–85; moral issue of,
    163–71, 171n2; reasons
    for/strategy of, ix–x, xii, xv–xvi,
    52–54, 60, 95, 97, 114–15, 119,
    123, 130, 132
Arabs, 7, 64
Army, British, 60–69, 69, 83, 129,
    152
Asquith, Herbert, 35
Australia, 122; after World War I, 2, 5,
    8, 9, 58, 128; in World War I, 2
Austria, 7, 102, 103, 107–9, 114,
    158
Austro-Hungarian Empire, 1, 2, 3, 7,
    110
Azerbaijan, 146–47

Backhouse, Sir Roger, 126, 127
Baldwin, Stanley, xiii, 34, 36, 58, 91,
    94, 95, 97–98, 170
Barnett, Correlli, 155n1
Battle of Britain, 63, 71, 72, 73, 155

Beck, Colonel Ludwig, 112

Beck, General, 139–40

Belgium, 102, 109, 151–54

Bene, Edvard, 114, 116

Blanning, T. C. W., 116

Blomberg, General von, 112

Blum, Leon, 21, 96, 100, 113

Bolsheviks, 7, 8

bombing, strategic, 69–70, 73–74, 92, 148

Bonnet, Georges, 141

Boutros-Gali, Boutros, xi

Britain: abdication of Edward VIII in, 21; class distinction in, 25–27; Conservative Party in, 29, 32, 34–36, 58, 83, 91; constitution of, 33, 37; Czechoslovakia and, 109–21, 122, 123, 130–31, 158–59, 160, 163–64; as democracy, 32; DRC of, 57–58; economy of, xii, xiv, 2, 8, 11, 12, 13, 15–16, 18, 25, 26, 27–31, 57–61, 63–64, 65–66, 69, 69, 71, 72–73, 79–80, 82–84, 85n1, 90, 91–95, 98, 100, 128, 145, 155, 159, 161–62; education in, 25–27, 63, 84; Empire of, 1, 38, 42, 54, 58–59, 60–61, 64, 89; France and, xii, 37, 39–43, 45, 47, 48, 49, 53–54, 65, 66, 70, 81, 94, 96–97, 101–2, 107–11, 111, 114–16, 118, 119–20, 122–23, 128–29, 132, 137–38, 139–42, 145, 151–54; French naval forces attacked by, 154; Germany as enemy of, 38–39, 41–43, 47–48, 52, 57–59, 60, 65, 69–70, 79, 82–85, 91–92, 107, 158–60; Germany/Austria and, 108–9, 114, 158; Hitler's desire for alliance with, 53–54; Hitler v., ix–x, xi–xii, 141, 155, 162; Italy and, 21–22, 59, 79, 80, 107–8,

128; Japan and, 7, 8–9, 10–12, 28, 58, 59, 60, 78, 79, 80, 82, 98–99, 134–36; Labour Party in, 29, 34–35, 53; Liberal Party in, 34–36, 90; Munich crisis/Agreements and, xv, 74, 100, 111, 116–24, 125; in 1930s, 24–38; Panama Canal and, xi; political system in, 32–38; religion in, 24–25, 34–35, 36, 88–89; as satisfied power, 37–38; shipbuilding industry in, 15–16; Spanish Civil War and, 95–97; Stressa agreement signed by, 21–22; Ten Year Rule in, 8, 57; U.S. and, 58, 115, 127, 135, 142n3; war declared on Germany by, ix, xii–xiii, xv, 141–42; at war with Germany, 93–94, 141–42, 145–52, 153–55, 160, 171; after World War I, xii, 1–2, 4–6, 7–16, 18, 159; in World War I, 93. See also Appeasement policy, British; Chamberlain, Neville; Churchill, William; military, British; Rearmament policy, British; United Kingdom

Bulgaria, 2

Bush, George W., 167–68

Canada, 2, 8, 9, 122, 165

Chamberlain, Annie (wife), 87, 88, 150

Chamberlain, Austen (half-brother), 89

Chamberlain, Ida (sister), 87, 92

Chamberlain, Joseph (father), 87, 89, 90

Chamberlain, Neville, 36, 66, 147; Appeasement policy of, blame placed on, xii, xiii–xiv, 136–37, 157–58, 159–61, 163, 165, 166–69, 170; Appeasement policy of, reasons for, xv–xvi, 60, 95, 97, 130; chief lieutenants of, 97–98; Churchill and, xiii, 91, 92, 97–98, 99–100, 121, 128, 142n3, 148–51; continental commitment and, 93, 129–30, 132–33; Czechoslovakia and, 112, 114, 116, 117–21, 122–24, 130–31; Daladier and, 49; death of, 150–51; as dominant political figure, xii–xiii; fascism and, 96–97; France and, 101–2; Germany/Hitler and, ix, xii–xiv, 58, 60, 69–70, 71, 72, 74, 79, 82, 84, 91–98, 101–5, 112, 114, 116, 117–21, 122–24, 128–30, 131–33, 139, 140–42, 155, 157, 159–61, 163, 165, 166, 170–71; Japan and, 58, 60, 98–99; life/career of, 87–91, 88; military support promised by, 131–33; Munich crisis/Agreements and, xv, 74, 100, 111, 116–24, 125; Mussolini meeting with, 128; Rearmament and, 58, 60, 64–65, 69–70, 71, 72, 74, 79, 82, 83, 84, 94–95, 122, 123, 132–33, 136; resignation of, 150; Soviet Union and, 132, 136–37, 139; Spanish Civil War and, 95–97; strategic priorities of, 92–94, 114–15, 123, 132; tax plan of, 94–95; U.S. and, 99–100; war avoidance as goal of, 89, 92, 94, 95, 114–15, 119, 123, 132, 137, 139, 140–41, 160–61, 166–67, 169, 170; war declared on Germany by, ix, xii–xiii, xv, 141–42

Chatfield, Lord, 78–80, 135

Chiang Kai-shek, 98

China, 9, 22–23, 98–99, 134–36

Christianity, 169–70

Churchill, William, 37; Appeasement policy opposed by, xiii, 125; Chamberlain, Neville, and, xiii, 91, 92, 97–98, 99–100, 121, 128, 142n3, 148–51; as Chancellor of Exchequer, 28; as first lord of Admiralty, 146–51, 147, 155n1; on German air force, 70–71; Hitler and, 149, 154; as prime minister, 150–51, 154–55; Ten Year Rule of, 8, 57; U.S. and, 142n3, 154, 155; war view of, 161

Civil War: American, xi; Spanish, 21, 22, 95–96, 134

class distinction, British, 25–27

Clayton-Bulwer Treaty, xi

Communism, 13, 16, 48, 49–50, 96, 136, 139, 166

Conservative Party, British, 29, 32, 34–36, 58, 83, 91

Constitution: Britain's unwritten, 33, 37; of U.S., 33

continental commitment, 93, 129–30, 132–33

Cooper, Duff, 121, 125

cruisers, battle, 76, 78, 80–81, 115

Cunningham, Sir Andrew, 127

Czechoslovakia, 7, 101, 103, 109–20, 122, 123; Britain and, 109–21, 122, 123, 130–31, 158–59, 160, 163–64; Chamberlain, Neville, and, 112, 114, 116, 117–21, 122–24, 130–31; France and, 109–11, 113, 114–18, 119, 120, 121–22; Germany and, 101, 103, 109–20, 122–23, 130–31, 158–59, 160, 163–64

Daladier, Edouard, 49, 111, 114–15, 121–22, 141, 170

Dalton, Hugh, 53

Defense Requirements Committee. *See* DRC

democracy: American, 12; Britain as, 32; German, 6; Great Depression and, 14; U.S. as, 12, 32

destroyers, 76, 81

disarmament: economics and, 13; German, 5–6, 7, 15, 51; London Naval Conference on, 14–16, 75, 83; Washington Naval Conference on, 10–12, 75, 78

Drax, Sir Plunkett, 137

DRC (Defense Requirements Committee), 57–58

Dreyfus Affair, 47

Dyer, Gwynne, 169

Eastern Europe, 41, 101–2, 109, 164

economy(ies): British, xii, xiv, 2, 8, 11, 12, 13, 15–16, 18, 25, 26, 27–31, 57–61, 63–64, 65–66, 69, 69, 71, 72–73, 79–80, 82–84, 85n1, 90, 91–95, 98, 100, 128, 145, 155, 159, 161–62; British military and, xiv, 57–61, 63–64, 65–66, 69, 69, 71, 72–73, 79–80, 82–84, 91–95, 98, 100, 159, 161–62; capitalist, 16–17; disarmament and, 13; French, xii, 18, 145; German, 4, 7, 13–15, 16, 18, 30, 31, 38, 83, 84, 103–4, 107, 130–31, 148; Great Depression impact on, xii, 14–18, 159; Hitler's policy on, 103–5; Jazz Age, 12–13; Soviet Union, 38; U.S., xi, 2, 8, 10, 12–13, 14–15, 17–18, 30, 31, 38, 84, 155; World War I debts/reparations and, 2–5, 8

Eden, Anthony, 63, 121, 125

education: in Britain, 25–27, 63, 84; in Germany, 84

Edward VII (king of England), 12

Edward VIII (king of England), 21, 36–37

Egypt, 78

Eisenhower, Dwight D., 166

Ethiopia, 21, 22, 23, 41, 52, 107

evil, xiv–xv, 165, 166, 168, 170

Expeditionary Force (British Army), 65, 129, 152

fascism: Chamberlain, Neville, and, 96–97; communism and, 96; in Italy, 13, 22, 59, 78, 96, 107; in Spain, 96, 107, 134

Finland, 146

Fisher, Sir Warren, 69–70

Four Year Plan, 104

France: armistice between Germany and, 154; Britain and, xii, 37, 39–43, 45, 47, 48, 49, 53–54, 65, 66, 70, 81, 94, 96–97, 101–2, 107–11, 111, 114–16, 118, 119–20, 122–23, 128–29, 132, 137–38, 139–42, 145, 151–54; British attack on, 154; British military defense of, 129, 151–54; Chamberlain, Neville, and, 101–2; Czechoslovakia and, 109–11, 113, 114–18, 119, 120, 121–22; Daladier as leader of, 49, 111, 114–15, 121–22, 141, 170; Dreyfus Affair in, 47; economy of, xii, 18, 145; German attack on, 128–29, 151–54; Germany and, 4–5, 38–48, 100–102, 108–16, 111, 118, 119–20, 121–23, 126–27, 128–29, 131–33, 134–42, 154, 158–59; Hitler v., ix–x, 100–102, 108–9, 113–14; Kellogg-Briand Pact by, 13; Leftist victory in, 21; Maginot Line of, 46; military of, 39, 42–48, 81, 84, 100–101, 111, 114–16, 141, 151–54, 161–62; Munich agreement signed by, 120, 121–22; in 1930s, 39–48; Rhineland and, 45, 52, 102, 103; Spanish Civil

War and, 95–97; U.S. and, 42,
153; war declared on Germany by,
141, 142; at war with Germany,
145, 151–54; after World War I,
4–5, 7, 10; in World War I, 2, 5,
43; World War II arms buildup by,
xiv

Franco, Francisco, 134
Fritsch, Baron von, 112

Gamelin, Maurice-Gustave, 45, 115,
121, 141, 152
Georges, General, 153
George V (king of England), 36
George VI (king of England), 37,
94–95, 150
Germany: armistice between France
and, 154; Austria and, 108–9,
114, 158; Britain at war with,
93–94, 141–42, 145–52, 153–55,
160, 171; Britain declaring war on,
ix, xii–xiii, xv, 141–42; British
military and, 52–54, 107, 108,
111, 114–16, 119, 132, 141–42,
151–54, 161–63; Chamberlain,
Neville, and, ix, xii–xiv, xiii–xiv,
58, 60, 69–70, 71, 72, 74, 79, 82,
84, 91–98, 101–5, 112, 114, 116,
117–21, 122–24, 128–30,
131–33, 139, 140–42, 155, 157,
159–61, 163, 165, 166, 170–71;
Czechoslovakia and, 101, 103,
109–20, 122–23, 130–31,
158–59, 160, 163–64; defeat of,
44; democracy in, 6; disarmament
of, 5–6, 7, 15, 51; economy of, 4,
7, 13–15, 16, 18, 30, 31, 38, 83,
84, 103–4, 107, 130–31, 148;
education in, 84; as enemy of
Britain, 38–39, 41–43, 47–48, 52,
57–59, 60, 65, 69–70, 79, 82–85,
91–92, 107, 158–60; evil of,
xiv–xv; expansion threatened by,

xii; France and, 4–5, 38–48,
100–102, 108–16, *111*, 118,
119–20, 121–23, 126–27,
128–29, 131–33, 134–42, 154,
158–59; France attacked by,
128–29, 151–54; France at war
with, 145, 151–54; Hindenburg as
president of, 49, 50; Italy and,
107–8, 119, 126, 127, 128, 134;
May-June 1940 victory of,
154–55, 157; in 1936, 49–54;
Norway and, 146, 147–49,
155n1; political parties in, 48–50;
rearmament by, 51–54, 83, 103,
107; as revisionist state, 37–38;
Soviet Union and, 132, 133, 134,
136–39, 140, 146–47, 148, 155,
162; Spanish Civil War and,
95–97, 134; Stressa agreement on,
21–22; Sudetenland occupied by,
109, 110, 116–22; war declared by
France on, 141, 142; Weimar
Republic in, 102; after World War
I, 3–7, 13–16, 18, 51; World War
I Allied victory over, 1, 43, 51,
111; World War I reparations and,
3–5. *See also* Hitler, Adolph;
military, German

Gibbs, N. H., 91
Goering, Hermann, 70, 104, *111,* 137
Gordon, Andrew, xiii–xiv
Gort, Lord, *153*
Great Britain. *See* Britain
Great Depression, xii, 14–18, 48, 159

Halifax, Lord, 97, 128, 131, 140, *147*
Harding, Warren G., 9–10
Heinlein, Conrad, 109, 114, 116–17
Hindenburg, Paul von, 49, 50
Hitler, Adolph, 21, 171n2; Allies v.,
112, 114, 116, 128, 131–33, 134,
145–55, 160, 161–65; Austria
and, 102, 103, 107–9, 114;

Britain v., ix–x, xi–xii, 141, 155, 162; British alliance sought by, 53–54; Chamberlain, Neville, and, xii, xiii–xiv, 58, 60, 69–70, 71, 72, 74, 79, 82, 84, 91–98, 101–5, 112, 114, 116, 117–21, 122–24, 128–30, 131–33, 139, 140–42, 155, 157, 159–61, 163, 165, 166, 170–71; Churchill and, 149, 154; confidence of, 105, 108; Czechoslovakia and, 101, 103, 109–20, 122, 123, 130–31, 158–59, 160, 163–64; economic policy of, 103–5; Four Year Plan of, 104; France v., ix–x, 100–102, 108–9, 113–14; on German air force, 70; German elites v., 112; Great Depression and, 16, 48; as insane/evil, xiv–xv, 157–58, 165, 166, 170; Mediterranean strategy against, 126–27, 134–35; Munich crisis/Agreements and, xv, 74, 100, *111*, 116–24, 125; Mussolini and, 22, 107–8, *111*, 119, 123, 128, 134; Poland invaded by, ix, xiii, xv, xvi, 131–34, 137–42, 145, 146, 158, 160; rearmament by, 51–54, 83, 103, 107; Rhineland reoccupied by, 45, 52, 102, 103; rise of, 14, 16, 18, 21, 40, 48–50, 65, 78; spending to keep pace with, 84; Stalin and, xv, 102, 128, 165; Sudetenland occupied by, 109, 110, 116–22; Treaty of Versailles and, 52, 110, 118; U.S. v., ix, 160; war blamed on, 145; weak points in dictatorship of, 102–5; West Wall of, 113–14; World War I resentment exploited by, 4, 5, 6. *See also* Germany; Holocaust
Hoare, Sir Samuel, 97–98
Holland, 126, 128–29, 151

Holocaust, xiv; Appeasement policy before, x, xii, xv, 163–65; Kristalnacht opening of, xv, 125–26
Hoover, Herbert, 13, 15
Hore-Belisha, Leslie, 66–67
Howard, Michael, 53
Hungary, 7, 109–10, 158, 166
Hurricane fighters, 73–74, 115

India, 59
Inskip, Sir Thomas, 70, 97–98
intelligence: British, 103, 116, 126, 132; French, 116; German, 112
Iraq, 6, 147, 167
Ireland, 1, 7, 8, 25, 32, 35. *See also* Northern Ireland
Italy: arms-production by, 46; Britain and, 21–22, 59, 79, 80, 107–8, 128; Egypt and, 78; Ethiopia and, 21, 22, 23, 41, 52, 107; expansion threatened by, xii; fascism in, 13, 22, 59, 78, 98, 107; Germany and, 107–8, 119, 126, 127, 128, 134; Locarno, 13; military of, 81; Munich agreement signed by, 120; as revisionist state, 37–38; in Spanish Civil War, 96, 134; Stressa agreement signed by, 21–22; after World War I, 7, 10; in World War I, 2, 107; World War II arms buildup by, xiv

Jackson, Julian, 141
Japan: Allies (World War II) and, 127; appeasement and, x; Britain and, 7, 8–9, 10–12, 28, 58, 59, 60, 78, 79, 80, 82, 98–99, 134–36; Chamberlain, Neville, and, 58, 60, 98–99; China and, 22–23, 98–99, 134–36; Manchuria invaded/occupied by, 22, 29, 58; Marco Polo Bridge incident by,

98–99; military of, 18, 22, 29, 58, 76, 78, 81, 82, 98–99, 135–36; Pearl Harbor attacked by, 18; as revisionist state, 37–38; U.S. and, 18, 99, 127, 135; after World War I, 5, 7, 8–13

Jazz Age, 12–13

Jews: Arabs v., 64; dislike of, 66–67; Eastern European, 164; Kristalnacht attack on, xv, 125–26; moral failure to protect, 164–65; on "Thou shalt not kill," 169–70. *See also* Holocaust

Kellogg-Briand Pact, 13
Kennedy, Paul, 38
Kiesling, Eugenia, 42
Kristallnacht, xv, 125–26

Labour Party (British), 29, 34–35, 53, 94, 150, 162
Laval, Pierre, 170
League of Nations, 6, 7, 18, 22–23, 110, 140
Liberal Party (British), 34–36, 90
Lloyd George, David, 1, 8, 35, 90
Locarno, Italy, 13
London Naval Conference, 14–16, 75, 83
Luftwaffe (German air force), 70–74, 104, 107, 115, 152, 155

MacDonald, Ramsey, xiii, 29, 58, 97
Maginot Line, 46
Manchuria, 22, 29, 58
mandate system (Treaty of Versailles), 5–6
Marco Polo Bridge incident, 98–99
Marlborough, Duke of, 61
Mediterranean strategy, 126–27, 134–35
methodical battle, tactic of, 43–44
Middle East, 59, 64

military: French, 39, 42–48, 81, 84, 100–101, 111, 114–16, 141, 151–54, 161–62; Italian, 81; Japanese, 18, 22, 29, 58, 76, 78, 81, 82, 98–99, 135–36; Soviet Union, 100

military, British: air defense/RAF in, 57, 60, 62, 66, 68–74, 69, 79, 82, 93–94, 98, 107, 115, 148, 155; Appeasement supported by, 84–85; British Army as, 60–69, 69, 83, 129, 152; Eastern Europe and, 41; economics and, xiv, 57–61, 63–64, 65–66, 69, 69, 71, 72–73, 79–80, 82–84, 91–95, 98, 100, 159, 161–62; Expeditionary Force of, 65, 129, 152; France defended by, 129, 151–54; Germany and, 52–54, 107, 108, 111, 114–16, 119, 132, 141–42, 151–54, 161–63; historians on, xiv; in inter-war period, 1, 6, 8, 9, 10–12, 14–16, 22, 28, 61–85; London Naval Conference and, 14–16, 75, 83; naval strategy/Royal Navy in, 66, 69, 71, 74–83, 93, 94, 98, 99, 107, 115, 119, 126–27, 135, 141–42, 146, 148, 149; parity, 70–71, 73, 80–81, 82, 115; priorities of, 64–66; Rearmament and, xiv, 57–85, 93–94, 107, 115, 155; Singapore Strategy of, 78, 86n15, 127; size of, 63–64; strategic bombing and, 69–70, 73–74, 92; Territorial Army of, 65, 66, 129–30, 146; warships, 75–77, 78–79, 80–83, 115, 141–42; Washington Naval Conference and, 10–12, 75, 78; in World War II, 31, 62–63, 151–54

military, German, 3, 4, 5, 6, 15, 43–44, 45, 46, 47, 48, 50–52, 54,

104, 107, 108–12, 113–15,
116–17, 120, 123–24, 151–52,
154–55; growing threat of, 65;
Luftwaffe (air force) of, 70–74,
104, 107, 115, 152, 155;
mechanization of, 67; navy in,
123–24; as untested, 133; in
World War II, 62–63
military, U.S.: in early 2000s, 84;
London Naval Conference and,
14–16, 83; Washington Naval
Conference and, 10–12, 75, 78;
after World War I, 9, 10–12,
14–16, 76, 81, 82
moral issue: of Allies (World War II),
160, 169; of war/appeasement,
163–71, 171n2
Munich crisis/Agreements, xv, 74,
100, 111, 116–24, 125
Mussolini, Benito, 21; Chamberlain,
Neville, meeting with, 128; Hitler
and, 22, 107–8, 111, 119, 123,
128, 134

Nazis. See Germany; Hitler, Adolph;
Holocaust
Neurath, Baron von, 112
New Zealand, 2, 8–9, 58, 128
Northern Ireland, 91
Norway, 146, 147–49, 155n1
nuclear war, 166

Ottoman Empire, 1

Pacific, U.S. in, 9–11, 18
Pact of Steel, 134
Palestine, 6, 7, 59, 64
Panama Canal, xi
parity, British military, 70–71, 73,
80–81, 82, 115
Pearl Harbor, Japanese attack on, 18
Pétain, Marshal Henri-Philippe,
153–54

Poland, 7, 101, 109–10; Hitler's
invasion of, ix, xiii, xv, xvi,
131–34, 137–42, 145, 146, 158,
160
Polanyi, Karl, 85n1
political system, British, 32–38
Pound, Sir Dudley, 127

radar systems, 31, 72, 115, 155
RAF (Royal Air Force), 60, 62, 98,
148; Rearmament of, 57, 66,
68–74, 69, 79, 82, 93–94, 107,
115, 155
rearmament, German, 51–54, 83,
103, 107
Rearmament policy, British, xiv, 57–85,
93–94, 107, 115, 155;
appropriateness of, 159; Cabinet
decision on, 57; Chamberlain,
Neville, and, 58, 60, 64–65,
69–70, 71, 72, 74, 79, 82, 83, 84,
94–95, 122, 123, 132–33, 136;
delay in, 83–85; as dual policy,
159, 160–61; in 1938, 107, 108;
of RAF, 57, 66, 68–74, 69, 79, 82,
93–94, 107, 115, 155; of Royal
Navy, 66, 69, 71, 74–83, 107
religion: in Britain, 24–25, 34–35, 36,
88–89; Christian, 169–70
revisionist states, 37–38
Reynaud, Paul, 153
Rhineland, 45, 52, 102, 103
Ribbentrop, Joachim von, 134, 137,
138
Romania, 163–64
Roosevelt, Franklin Delano, 17, 99,
154
Royal Air Force. See RAF
Royal Navy (British), 119, 126–27,
135, 146, 148, 149; Rearmament
of, 66, 69, 71, 74–83, 107;
warships, 75–77, 78–79, 80–83,
115, 141–42

Russia, 7; Bolshevik revolutionaries in, 7, 8; Stalin as leader of, xv, 13, 17, 21, 100, 101, 102, *117*, 128, 136–38, 139, 165; in World War I, 2

satisfied power, Britain as, 37–38
Schuschnigg (Austrian prime minister), 108
Serbia, 2, 3
shipbuilding industry (British), 15–16
Simon, Sir John, 97
Simpson, Wallis, 36
Singapore Strategy, 78, 86n15, 127
socialism, 22, 48
Somerville, Sir James, 154
South Africa, 5, 122
Soviet Union, xiv, 18, 37, 59, 96, 123; arms-production by, 46; Chamberlain, Neville, and, 132, 136–37, 139; collapse of, 110; economy of, 38; Germany and, 132, 133, 134, 136–39, 140, 146–47, 148, 155, 162; military of, 100. *See also* Russia
Spain: Civil War in, 21, 22, 95–96, 134; fascism in, 96, 107, 134
Spitfire fighters, 73–74
Stalin, Joseph, 13, 17, 21, 100, 101, *117*, 136–38, 139; Hitler and, xv, 102, 128, 165
submarines, 76
Sweden, 146, 147

tax plan, of Chamberlain, Neville, 94–95
Ten Year Rule, 8, 57
Territorial Army (British), 65, 66, 129–30, 146
Treaty of Versailles, 2, 3, 5–7, 12, 15, 22, 51, 52, 101; Hitler and, 52, 110, 118
Trenchard, Lord, 68–69

Trent (merchant ship), xi
Turkey, 7, 8
Turkish Army, 2

United Kingdom: defense of, 64–65, 71, 74–75, 77–79; as trading nation, xiv, 30; as U.S. economic satellite, 155. *See also* Britain; Ireland
United Nations, xi
United States. *See* U.S.
U.S. (United States): appeasement and, x–xi, 115; Boutros-Gali ousted by, xi; Britain and, 58, 115, 127, 135, 142n3; Chamberlain, Neville, and, 99–100; Churchill and, 142n3, 154, 155; Civil War in, xi; Constitution of, 33; democracy in, 12, 32; economy, xi, 2, 8, 10, 12–13, 14–15, 17–18, 30, 31, 38, 84, 155; flip-flops by, 167–68; France and, 42, 153; Hitler v., ix, 160; Hungary and, 166, 167; in Iraq War of 2003, 167; isolationist stance of, 18; Japan and, 18, 99, 127, 135; Jazz Age in, 12–13; Jews refused entry to, 165; Kellogg-Briand Pact by, 13; League of Nations and, 23; in Pacific, 9–11, 18; Panama Canal built by, xi; in Vietnam, 167; Washington Naval Conference and, 10–12, 75, 78; after World War I, 2, 5, 7, 8–15, 17–18; in World War I, 2. *See also* military, U.S.

Versailles. *See* Treaty of Versailles
Victoria (queen of England), 12
Vietnam, 167
Voroshilov, Kliment, 139

war: avoidance by Chamberlain, Neville, 89, 92, 94, 95, 114–15,

119, 123, 132, 137, 139, 140–41,
160–61, 166–67, 169, 170;
Churchill's view of, 161; hawk
view on, 161–62; as just, 161,
168–70; moral issue of, 163–71,
171n2
warships, British, 75–77, 78–79,
80–83, 115, 141–42
Washington Naval Conference,
10–12, 75, 78
Weimar Republic, 102
Wellington, Duke of, 61–62
West Wall, 113–14
Wilson, Woodrow, 7, 10
Women, voting rights of, 32
World War I: Allies, reparations
ordered by, 2–5; Allies, victory of,
1–2, 43, 51; armistice ending, 1,
7; Australia after, 2, 5, 8, 9, 58,
128; Australia in, 2; Austro-
Hungarian forces in, 2, 3; Britain
after, xii, 1–2, 4–6, 7–16, 18,
159; Britain in, 93; death tolls in,
2; debts, 2–5, 8; France after, 4–5,
7, 10; France in, 2, 5, 43;
Germany after, 3–7, 13–16, 18,

51; Germany in, defeat of, 1, 43,
51, 111; Italy after, 7, 10; Italy in,
2, 107; Japan after, 5, 7, 8–13;
New Zealand after, 8–9, 128;
New Zealand in, 2; resentment
exploited by Hitler, 4, 5, 6; Russia
in, 2; Serbia in, 2, 3; Treaty of
Versailles ending, 2, 3, 5–7, 12,
15, 22, 51, 52, 101, 110, 118;
Turkish Army in, 2; twenty-year
truce following, 1–18; U.S after,
2, 5, 7, 8–15, 17–18; U.S. in, 2;
U.S. military after, 9, 10–12,
14–16, 76, 81, 82
World War II: Allies, Hitler v., 112,
114, 116, 128, 131–33, 134,
145–55, 160, 161–65; Allies,
Japan and, 127; Allies, moral
credibility of, 160, 169; arms
buildup, xiv; British military in, 31,
62–63, 151–54; German military
in, 62–63; as just war, 168–69;
"nightmare scenario" of, 136
World War III, 166

Yugoslavia, 7, 101

About the Author

James Levy received his Ph.D. from the University of Wales Swansea. He is the author of *The Royal Navy's Home Fleet in World War II* and has published articles in *The Mariner's Mirror, Naval War College Review,* and *The Journal of Strategic Studies.* Currently, he holds the position of Special Assistant Professor at Hofstra University, and lives on Long Island with his wife and two children.